Not
Dead
Yet

Not Dead Yet

The column that challenges ageism and
celebrates being 50-plus

With an Introduction by Philip Howard

Cartoons by Neil Bennett

TIMES BOOKS

HarperCollinsPublishers
77–85 Fulham Palace Road
Hammersmith
London W6 9JB

The HarperCollins website address is
www.**fire**and**water**.com

First published 2003

Reprint 10 9 8 7 6 5 4 3 2 1

© Times Newspapers Ltd 2003

© Cartoons Neil Bennett

ISBN 0 00 716674 5

The Times is a registered trademark of Times Newspapers Ltd

British Library Cataloguing in Publication Data
A catalogue record for this book is available from
the British Library

Text compilation and design by Clare Crawford

Printed and bound in Great Britain by
Clays Ltd, St Ives plc

INTRODUCTION

by

Philip Howard

Old age is the last taboo. Our cult of youth in the United Kingdom and the United States has made senescence the unmentionable disease. For other conditions, society has become more tolerant. To discriminate against others because of their race, sex, sexual orientation, class, religion, colour, intelligence (or lack of it), size or any other peculiarity has become politically incorrect. It is even deemed insensitive to describe a condition as a "handicap". "Downsizing" is the modern euphemism of employers who manage their "human resources" badly for sacking older workers in order to replace them with younger (and cheaper, and possibly less useful) workers. The sole attribute that is still unforgivable is growing old.

This modern prejudice is novel. Previous generations worshipped sages from Ezekiel and Sophocles to Bertrand Russell and Bernard Shaw, the Queen Mother and Bob Hope. The Victorian paterfamilias hung on to power and inheritance to his last gasp. The GOM ("Grand Old Man") Gladstone was Prime Minister at the age of 83. And the Prince of Wales had to waste his life in idleness, until he inherited the less demanding job of the throne as Edward VII, at the youthful age of 60, from his mother, the octogenarian imperial icon. Other nations do not share our aversion to wrinklies. Matriarchal Mommas still rule Italian families, OK? Politicians do not become statesmen or prime ministers in Greece or China until they at least reach their prime at 60.

But in our neophiliac world of mayfly celebrity, billions of dollars and pounds are wasted on magical potions supposed to retard the signs of ageing. Nothing new in that. In one of the oldest myths, the witch Medea rejuvenates Jason and his aged father. She then punishes the usurper King Pelias by persuading his daughters to cut him up and boil him, in order to make him young again. Ageism is stupid as well as offensive. Get you to my lady's chamber and tell her, let her Botox an inch thick, to this favour most of us hope to come, and increasing numbers of us manage it. Whatever our age, we are all fellow-travellers on our Ship of Fools towards the few certainties of existence.

The stereotypes of age are as broad-brushed imprecise as most generalisations about humanity. Old men (and women too) are not necessarily wise just because they have seen more of life. Nor are they necessarily irritable, stuffy, miserly and prejudiced against change, as oldies are reputed to be. The young can be judicious as well as cool. When jeered at in the House of Commons for his youth, William Pitt (aged 33) replied: "The atrocious crime of being a young man I shall neither attempt to palliate nor deny."

There are signs that we are recognising the wicked waste of writing off our grey tigers and tigresses, just because they are senior citizens or "crumblies" or "concessions", or whatever the euphemism of this month happens to be. Legislation in some countries prohibits age discrimination in job advertisements, as it already bans race and gender discrimination. Ageist jokes are becoming as unfunny as racist or sexist jokes. He's so old that he was DJ at the Boston Tea Party? Not even the most rednosed comedian on the northern club circuit today would tell the story of the old guy who goes to the doctor's and the doctor says, "I've got bad news and I've got worse news. The bad news is you've got Alzheimer's. The worse news is you've got inoperable cancer and you'll be dead in two months." And the old man replies, "Well, at least I don't have Alzheimer's."

The most promising sign of the decline in idiotic prejudice is the "Not Dead Yet" column in *The Times* on Tuesdays. This records the outrageous, funny and encouraging remarks of the week on age. You do not have to be old to enjoy the jokes or groan at the folly. Children and centenarians will both laugh at the witty illustrations by Neil Bennett for our collection. "Not Dead Yet" is helping to make society more tolerant and wiser, as well as entertaining us. It is time that we grew up. Bernard Baruch, the office boy who became an adviser to presidents and Winston Churchill, got it right: "I will never be an old man. Old age is always fifteen years older than I am." Right on, young man.

Philip Howard, August 2003

2001

9 JANUARY 2001

"At 67 Bobby Robson can still get excited."
GMTV sports reporter when Newcastle United scored an equaliser against Manchester United

"My job dictates that I don't really get out much, so to be in a crowded theatre with lots of old people is quite frightening. Surrounded by men in tartan trousers and bifocals and women whose last orgasm coincided with the Suez crisis, it was like being in the waiting room for heaven."
Guardian TV critic Gareth McLean

"I was looking at the funeral business the other day and it's interesting because we're all scared of it. Nobody ever negotiates a price. I found out that a coffin costs £37 from the factory and the cheapest you can buy from a funeral director is £4,000. So, there's room for somebody to do really well."
Simon Woodroffe, founder of the YO! Sushi empire

To secure its re-election, the Government should send £1,000 to six million of the poorest pensioners"
Frederick Forsyth, author of The Day of the Jackal

"I don't cook any more. No one in their right mind does. People complain that young people no longer know how to, but I say good. No one weaves their own cloth these days either."
Shirley Conran

16 JANUARY 2001

The phone rang. "We are doing a survey about use of the internet. May I ask you some questions?"
   "Yes."
   "First of all, how old are you?"
   "69."
   "You're too old. Thank you for your time. Goodbye."
Tony Greenfield, Little Hucklow, Derbyshire

I think it's great to have been a child of the Sixties. We had the best music, which remains unsurpassed. We had plenty to say politically – the teenage uprising against Vietnam and nuclear war was protest from the heart and it worked. We shook off the trepidation and caution of our parents' postwar terror of enjoying themselves in case they might be damned in the next world. We rocked. I still wear jeans and yes, my bum looks big in them but then my bum looked big in 1965. I went to hear the Stones at Wembley two years ago and I could have shut my eyes and been in Hyde Park in '64. My children don't think I'm sad – I always told my eldest son that I had an L-plate on my back. We should be pleased with ourselves. Here we are, still trucking and giving life some stick.
Julia Richardson, Oxford

Ten years ago five of us, all over 50 and some nearer 60, started playing guitar and singing together. Now, as the Old

Boy Network, we are having the time of our lives playing all the good stuff from the Sixties, doing gigs for charities and for fun. Not so many groupies as we would like, but then we are pretty whacked out at the end of the evening so it's probably nature's way.
Chris Bailey, Westerham, Kent

I am 56, a keen motorcyclist and still driving a speedboat, as well as being involved in teaching Scouts to sail. I have a car, which is boring but necessary for business. The only way I know I am getting old is that my birthday suit requires ironing.
Allan Glass, Holbury, New Forest

What a rose-tinted, Panglossian picture has been painted for the over-50s – a time full of leisure and wonderful new opportunities. However much we may try to enthuse about the joys of the second half-century, it is nevertheless a period of decline, of withdrawal and giving things up, of illness and infirmities, of slowing down, of losing one's partner and friends. No doubt there are many men and women – especially women – who can adapt to a life of leisure as easily as a yuppie takes to a Porsche, but for many hundreds of others the season of superannuation is a dismal, depressing time with little to look forward to.
John Copeland, Burton, Lincolnshire

Quote from number two son: "Dad, age is only a collection of numbers."
David Batterbury, Brentwood, Essex

23 JANUARY 2001

If all goes to plan, and despite post-twentysomething decrepitude, in 18 months I shall begin a career as a newly qualified nurse – just after my fiftieth birthday.
Stephen Gee, Wolverhampton

A few years ago I was chairing a bench of lay magistrates and an 18-year-old, liable to a driving disqualification, was explaining why he should be given another chance. He said: "Each week I drive my elderly parents to the shops." "How old are they?" I asked. "Dad's 42 and Mum's 41," he replied.
Ian Sampson, Walton-on-Thames, Surrey

Most tourists are so unadventurous they huddle around airports, hotels and resort beaches – the rest of us don't have to go far to escape.
Tony Wheeler, the 53-year-old publisher of Lonely Planet guidebooks

I am 86, still drive a car and even published a book last year. But I knew I was getting on a bit when I caught myself pouring sugar into the ashtray instead of the coffee cup.
Gerd Sommerhoff, OBE, Cambridge

Last year a friend and I (both fifty-plus) went on a driving holiday to Spain. We booked nothing, not even the ferry. We had three brilliant weeks, spending nights at campsites from San Sebastian to Barcelona in a tent bought for £25 at Asda. Doing it again this year. She told me: "Live the rest of your life as if your hair is on fire."
David Gould, Watford, Hertfordshire

Overheard: "Yes, Grandad is old, but only on the outside."
Geoffrey Bubb, Kingswinford, West Midlands

I am 86 years young, an active governor of two local primary schools, which I visit weekly to help. I recently received an award from the borough for "helping to raise the standard of maths in the infant school". In addition, I am the sole and full-time carer of my husband (a mere 83) who has suffered from Parkinson's disease for 15 years. We follow the motto "one can't help growing older but there is no need to be old". Contrary to the modern trend, we have never sued anyone and we are not ashamed to hold hands in public.
Dr Julia Matthews, Bexleyheath, Kent

Alan Greenspan, the 74-year-old chairman of the Federal Reserve Board – he fixes the American interest rate – was living with Andrea Mitchell for 12 years before he asked her to marry him. "I should have done it sooner," he confessed – he was 70.
The Sunday Times

"When you get to my age you either run away or jump in with both feet."
Jan Leeming, 59

30 JANUARY 2001

Chatting last year with some children at the primary school where I am a volunteer, I was asked my age. When I told them I was 72, one child asked, "Are you still alive?" I wondered if I should get a second opinion.
Mary Blumenau, London

I am going to carry on colouring my hair, wearing diamonds and painting my nails until the day I die.
Jenni Murray, presenter of Woman's Hour

A tall, good looking young West Indian – as he accidentally brushed against me on a train – said: "That's a tight, hard ass for an old girl." I'm 64. He made my day. He made my year.
Catherine White, Bexleyheath, Kent

Recently I responded to a request for blood donors. I filled out the forms about my sex life (I wish) and my medical history. When called to the desk expecting my thumb to be pricked, I was told condescendingly: "We don't take blood from the over-sixties."
Maurice Simove (1939 model) Cardiff

"Cash's performances are so deeply felt, so pure, so right, you wish you could pass a law to force everyone to hear them."
Review of 69-year-old Johnny Cash's latest album, Solitary Man

When I was six years old I asked my late (and she made late an art) mother on her approaching birthday, in order to get her card correct. "Are you going to be 36 or 63?"
Viscount Simon, House of Lords

At our age most people are retiring, but we are just getting into gear.
Gordon Taylor, 65, and Guy Cooper, 66, presenters of The Curious Gardeners, a new BBC2 programme based on the Two Fat Ladies formula

6 FEBRUARY 2001

Four years ago I discovered I had prostate cancer. A routine blood test revealed the bad news early enough for me to have brachytherapy treatment, in which the gland is injected with radioactive seeds that destroy the cancer cells. I am celebrating my total recovery by giving myself a treat of which Walter Mitty would have been proud: on the eve of my 70th birthday, I am going to conduct the Philharmonia Orchestra

and a 600-strong choir at the Royal Albert Hall. Proceeds are going to the Prostate Research Campaign UK and I would be especially happy to welcome *Times* readers.
Humphrey Burton CBE, London. Royal Albert Hall

Some truths about ageing: Things you buy now won't wear out. You can have a party and the neighbours won't even notice. Your secrets are safe with your friends, because they won't remember them.
Mike and Pam Bird, Kingsdown, Bristol

In a recent game of rugby between golden oldies, a 65-year-old hooker was playing his last game, so the opposing captains agreed to let him score a try. He was duly allowed to catch the ball and set off at a slow gallop into the opponents' half, while bodies deftly dived out of his way. Alas, he eventually ran out of steam, whereupon a player from each side lifted him up and carried him over the try line.
Bill Newham, Worsley, Manchester

In Phoenix recently, I went into a travel agent to book a flight to San Francisco. The agent patiently took time to book the best deal and asked for my passport. "Holy cow," she said, "you're 67!" and promptly entered my age. The new fare was half the price.
Ron Scarborough, Lowestoft, Suffolk

My favourite lesson came from a friend's granddaughter: "Granny says she was going to grow old gracefully but she's left it too late."
Christine Kelly, Cowes, Isle of Wight

13 FEBRUARY 2001

Keeping supple is the secret of a youthful older age as Joan Collins, 67, demonstrates. The mother of three, who is a size 8 and boasts a 27-inch waist, was taught how to do the splits by her grandmother. "I have exercised and kept supple all my life," she says.

Twiggy has joined NDY's happy band and, like many people entering their second half-century, is embarking on a new career – launching a new skincare range called Aroma Therapies for Face and Mind. Her products contain natural ingredients such as geranium and ylang ylang. All are perfect for men too except, maybe, the eye make-up remover.

The white-haired guide arrived during a school visit to the Roman fort at Housesteads, between Newcastle and Carlisle, and a small voice said: "Is that one of the Romans?"
Stan Walton, Sunderland, Tyne and Wear

Studying the photograph of Michelangelo's *David*, even without my reading specs, I am convinced that the main difference between us is that I have a pair of trunks.
Jim Jefferies (70-plus), Childwall, Liverpool

Now in my seventieth year I become ever more mindful of my late father's advice: "After 70, a pound saved is a pound wasted . . ."
Stanley Blenkinsop, Macclesfield, Cheshire

On our round of library services to the housebound, we are welcomed by a 94-year-old lady with cakes she makes herself. Always alert and sprightly, one day she admitted she was slowing down and added: "Oh to be 80 again."
Marian Shearan, Gravesend, Kent

20 FEBRUARY 2001

I recently attended my son's wedding in New York as his best man, five days after my 80th birthday. On a whim I wrote to Guinness World Records and now have a certificate to prove I am the proud record holder as the world's oldest best man.
Pat Spooner, Guildford, Surrey

The Mirror declined to review my memoir, *Legless but Smiling*, about my climbing experiences on artificial legs, on the ground that "you are a little old for our target market". I am 60.
Norman Croucher OBE, Topsham, Devon

I read your page while drinking a large mug of tea after a bike ride home from work followed by a three-mile run (well, jog). I am only 60 but sadly, unlike Joan Collins, I am unable to do the splits. But then I couldn't at 20 anyway.
Coleene Tudor, Hereford

I missed a lecture recently and asked a couple of friends aged 83 and 84 if they could tell me something of what it was about. "Sorry," said the 84-year-old cheerfully, "We can't help you there. She can't hear and I can't remember."
Elizabeth Urch, Pitlochry

How, when you are 50, do you escape the mutton-dressed-as-lamb syndrome and not fall into the trap of walking about clothed like a dead sheep?
Jessie Roy, Belfast

The answer? From the New York fashion shows Joanna Coles reports: "Few names in the frock business inspire more loyalty in the mature customer than Halston."

Thirty-five years ago, at the age of 32, I joined a keep-fit class. The remarkable thing is that the class is still run by the same lady, who is now 90. In spite of her age, she is able to do all the exercises with us.
Joan Watkins, Malvern, Worcester

27 FEBRUARY 2001

It is all down to our genes. If you are born a dour, boring individual then the chances are that is how you will be in later life. I am approaching 57 and although my car appears to be getting lower and I don't do things quite as fast as I did, I still give life my best shot. That is why riding my motorcycle is such a joy. The freedom I get keeps me going. It is my two fingers to all I loathe and despise in society and the thumbs-up to life.
Karrol Smulovic, Brackley, Northamptonshire

Although I had never used a computer, or even typed before, I decided it was time I joined the modern world and corresponded by e-mail. I told one of my daughters: "I thought I would buy a laptop so that when I get older the grandchildren don't think I'm stupid." What came back was not what I expected to hear: "But you are already old." A few weeks before, I had sailed my boat back single-handed from St Malo to Southampton.
Julia Twyman, Faversham, Kent

"In their eyes any man of 53 who can 'pull' a companion as glamorous as Nancy Dell'Olio, said to be nudging 40, must have a certain style."
The Sunday Times Magazine on the attitude of England fans to Sven-Goran Eriksson

6 MARCH 2001

After a motorcycle accident in the Nevada desert, Lauren Hutton, 57, the former model, has had titanium holding together her right leg and right arm and she is in constant pain. Yet the game old trout says all she really fears is "not finding someone to love".
Peter McKay, Daily Mail

"What 51-year-old single woman would have turned down Lord Archer's invitation to go to South Africa?"
Nikki Kingdon's second husband in The Sunday Times

I parked my car in Manchester on the day of a visit from the Queen and told the parking meter attendant that when I was a schoolboy at a local grammar school, on the day of The Queen's visit we were made to line the pavements and wave as she drove past. He asked if that was Queen Victoria.
Dr Eric F. Marks (aged 64), Manchester

At 52 and while receiving sympathetic diagnostic treatment for a potential prostate problem, the young urologist, considering options, said: "I don't suppose you are worried about fertility now." My new baby daughter had been born the day before.
David Hitchens, Downpatrick, N Ireland

A few weeks before my mother-in-law unexpectedly died in her 90th year, the family finally persuaded her that she really could afford the nursing home care that she clearly needed. The dear independent lady had argued about the expense, saying her investments were to be saved for old age.
Nigel Hall, Sheffield

As I waited for my train at Waterloo, an elderly gentleman asked if I would confirm the platform number for a Guildford train. We talked and he brightly told me he was ending his five-day week commuting for, at 87, he was finding it too tiring and frustrating travelling to and from the City. As we walked to the train and with a 20-plus advantage in years, I was filled with a new lease of life.
Malcolm McIntyre, West Clandon, Surrey

13 MARCH 2001

Your children may not approve, but Slapper Productions put on risqué shows that go down well with NDY types. Sample humour: "Approaching her fifties, a chick from the Sixties/Is driven to acts of great folly/Her short skirt denies the width of her thighs/And she weeps for the late Buddy Holly." OK, it is sexist but they are pre-PC. Pulling the strings are Pat Rice and Marianne Stork. Being manipulated are Peter Hughes and Ian Hardy, all from Cookham, near Maidenhead.

Half-term holiday. Grandchildren discuss which video to watch. We adults are concerned at the various ratings for different age

groups. A film is suggested. Jack, aged eight, opines:
"Grandma can't see that. They say mother-f." I am so glad he
is looking after me.
Mrs C. Kevin, Banstead, Surrey

There is a new party person in town. The It girl is dead; long
live the practically pensionable party animal. Yes, it is the
greying babe, or Greybe. Step forward Cilla Black, 57, style
icon.
The Sunday Times

In 1963 I was appointed as paymaster to the 1st Battalion the
King's Regiment, then in Berlin. I overheard two subalterns
discussing my arrival. "Who is the old boy who's just joined
us?" I was 41.
Major L. Berker, Kidderminster

I am mindful of my late father's *obiter dicta*. On summer
Saturday afternoons when I would have preferred cricket, he
took me through the Talmudic tractate, the Ethics of the
Fathers. As I reached 70, I delighted to have the "hoary head"
so ascribed to a 70-year-old in the Ethics. And am gratified that
as I approach 80 I might anticipate "the gift of special strength",
so ascribed to an 80-year-old. After a severe heart attack and
hip replacement, it will be welcome.
Ansel Harris, London NW3

Upon my nest becoming empty, I put on my dream list:
Terracotta Warriors, fishing for salmon, Victoria Falls, the Inca
Trail, crossing the Rockies by train, India's temples,
Cambodia's ancient architecture. My dream now is to find a
travel company looking for an older but determined lady to
send around the world to assess destinations for gadabout
crinklies.
Mrs Pauline Redwood, Leicester

20 MARCH 2001

What's the difference between Giorgio Armani and Roberto Cavalli? Both are Italian, both are fashion designers with stores in Paris, Milan and New York, and both are the wrong side of 60.
The Telegraph Magazine

A cousin, in her late eighties, was asked if she would be interested in Meals-on-Wheels. As a lifelong worker with the Salvation Army, she said that she'd be glad to help. She was somewhat insulted to find that she was the one being offered the meals.
Joanna Livingston, Belvedere, Kent

I think I wanted to skip childhood and get to adulthood. I still do. I can't wait to be old. I just think I'll really enjoy it.
The playwright Conor McPherson

About ten years ago, when I was 40, I took part in a local fun run. I was surprised to see an elderly man of my acquaintance

lining up with all the much younger competitors. Knowing that he was in his early seventies, to my shame I allowed myself a silent scoff at his audacity. Minutes later he disappeared into the distance in front of me, taking my morale with him.
Dr William Holmes, Enniskillen, Co Fermanagh

Robin, a losing contestant on *The Weakest Link*, commented in his interview: "I hope Gill doesn't win because she is too old to enjoy the prize money."
Marian Gale-Batten, Overijse, Brussels

A few years ago, just turned 50, I was asked to model for a hotel brochure. Feeling impressed with myself, I tripped through the hotel foyer and asked the young lift attendant to take me to the suite where, I emphasised, I was to be photographed. He looked quizzically at me and said: "Did you used to be good-looking then?"
Coral Thomas, Baldrine, Isle of Man

After being knocked down by a car I was on a trolley in A&E for six hours. At the third time of being asked my age, I was tempted to reply 55 – but I'd aged 20 years waiting to be seen.
Mr C. H. Brown, Saltdean, East Sussex

27 MARCH 2001

When I meet older fans I swear that I can see the girls they were – the wrinkles vanish. That so many people respond to me is fabulous. It is like having a kind of Alzheimer's disease, where everyone knows you and you don't know anyone.
Tony Curtis, 75

My 14-year-old daughter and I had a battle over new shoes. Her fashionable wishes did not accord with my knowledge that her feet had not stopped growing and could be damaged by high heels. "It must be lovely," she said, "to be so old that you don't care how you look any more."
Sue Howe, Balcombe, Sussex

I see being a good granny – without being an interfering granny – as every bit as important as being creative. Passing love and warmth down the generations is probably the most important thing any human being can do.
Pat Barker, novelist, 57

As a drama specialist of 56 I am constantly amused by children's perceptions of age. In role plays of older people the children portray toothless, crippled, stereotypes supported by walking sticks who they tell me are 40 or 50 years old.
Carolyn Drury, Nearly Instant Theatre Session, Newark, Notts

I am approaching my three-quarter century in July, and I was making a purchase in a local shop this week. As the salesgirl was about to ring it up on the till, I asked for the pensioners' discount. "Oh", she said blithely, "I didn't know whether you were a pensioner or just a 28-year-old after a hard night."
The Rev Canon Elizabeth Kilbourn-Mackie, Warminster

When my wife and I reached 70, we decided to have the kitchen remodelled, including having a wood floor. When she was told of this, a friend said: "Do you think it wise? At your age will you get the use out of it?"
Bruce Wall, Taunton, Somerset

I admitted that the thought of being 30 had so terrified me that I had altered my birthdate in *Who's Who* to lose a year. I soon realised the folly of this and today I don't cheat about my age. I boast about it. There is a great sense of liberation in daring to be oneself. If one does so, one discovers hidden strengths one did know one had.
Barbara Castle, 90

3 APRIL 2001

In M&S food hall in Truro last Monday, two sales ladies walked past me. One nudged the other and asked me: "Were you one of the *Likely Lads* on television?" "Mmmmm," I replied. The second one said: "Oh, I thought so. That ages me, doesn't it?" . . . sigh!
Rodney Bewes, by e-mail

For the past 20 years or so I have very much enjoyed running, and now that I have turned 60 I fully intend to continue as long as possible. While out training recently, I had to pass a noisy group of youths who volunteered the following: "Yes, it's a lass, but you've no chance – she's at least 40." Little did they know they had made my evening.
Hetta Morath, by e-mail

The beauties of yesterday become muttering, mad old women.
Anthony Powell in A Writer's Notebook

Men over the age of 50 are being recruited for the world's first "man band". They will be moulded, on television, to become a sort of pre-geriatric Hear'Say, in a riposte to the cult of youth. Hundreds of middle-aged wannabes, all prepared to face public humiliation, have applied.
Evening Standard

"All 50-year-olds need a bit of help and I am five years older than the Hall"
Joanna Lumley, announcing plans for a gala concert to celebrate the 50th anniversary of the Royal Festival Hall

In her tradition of arranged marriages, there is no slur about being with an older man. They tend to choose an older man who has got something, rather than just a randy young squire.
Wilbur Smith on marrying his 30-year-old Muslim wife, 38 years his junior

10 APRIL 2001

A golfing chum in his mid-sixties, a retired vet and fit as a fiddle, had his offer to help in the foot-and-mouth crisis turned down despite the reported shortage of vets. At the same time my brother-in-law, also in his mid-sixties and a GP, is being

bribed by the Government to stay in practice because of the
shortage of doctors.
Marcus Wild, Shutford, Oxfordshire

Don't delay, or they will steal your money. I retired last year at
60. I did not immediately collect my pension. When I attempted
to do so 11 months later I was told they would refund only
three months of the entitlement plus a minimum level of
interest on the outstanding eight months. The majority of the
entitlement is retained by the Government. No argument; no
explanation. That is the law. Write to your MP, they said
helpfully. I can find no rationale for this theft. It must add up to
quite a windfall for the DSS. Has anyone else had a similar
experience? Anyone trying to change the law? I tried to reach
the Pensions Review Team, but after 20 minutes on hold, I
gave up.
Jane Stead, Birmingham

As I put on a lovely blue scarf I have had since the Sixties, my
18-year-old daughter said, "Can I have that scarf when you
die?"
Lynda Last, 52, Huddersfield

My late husband Bernard Braden used to say: "The human
brain is the most sophisticated and complex computer in the
world – it only ceases to function when you get up to speak in
public." I have become increasingly aware that there are many
people who have something to say but lack the confidence to
say it in public, and have started a new company called
Speakerpower. The team of tutors includes David Jacobs,
Sylvia Sims, Miriam Karlin, Jane Lapotaire and Jan Leeming.
Barbara Kelly, 76, London NW3

At a Royal Air Force reunion an octogenarian, who was an ace
pilot during the Second World War, asked me if I remembered
the bromide that was put in the tea when we were young

trainees and, at my affirmative, he went on: "Well, I think it is beginning to work."
Wing Commander D. O. Luke, Thurlestone, Devon

17 APRIL 2001

When I retired at 60 I decided to learn to tap dance. I have been tapping now for ten years with a group of ladies from 50 to 80. We love it and it keeps us fit.
Amy Rich, Liverpool

My wife and I attended the burial of a 91-year-old woman in Aberdeen. At the top of the family gravestone were the words "Be ye also ready". Later we commented on this stern behest to the woman's elder brother. Jock Gaffron cocked an impish eye: "T' hell wi that, I've a lot o' damage still to do." Jock died last April, aged 103. The last surviving Gordon Highlander of the First World War, he lost a leg on the Somme when he was 19.
W. D. Hall, Methven

Just in case you're a round-faced lawyer on the less popular side of 40, if your stylist suggests a Fanni cut, think again.
The Sunday Times

C. S. Lewis got it right when he said: "I don't think that age matters so much as people think. Parts of me are still 12 and I think other parts were already 50 when I was 12."
Robert Woolley, Long Buckby, Northampton

It was suggested to my Great Aunt Lizzie, 92, that a little whisky in her last drink at night might help her sleeping problems. She replied: "I wouldn't like to, dear – it might get me into bad habits."
Elizabeth Gold, Woodbridge, Suffolk

John Boorman has always made accessible, mainstream movies but used them to say something more interesting and original – something a shade darker – than you might expect. This is why, at 68, he is still a compelling film-maker.
The Daily Telegraph

Spotted on the back of a minibus in Perthshire, a sticker saying: "Be nice to your kids, they choose your nursing home."
Christopher Hope, Edinburgh

I am the director of a welfare service with a staff of varied ages, ranging from 25 to my secretary, who is a brilliant 71. Those of us over 50 have been blessed with an education that included tables, precis and comprehension. So I was affronted when a young staff member accused the service of being menopausal. Yes, I replied, that's probably true – but at least we can spell it.
Sandie Saunders, British Red Cross, London

24 APRIL 2001

My mother died in her sleep aged 99 having being a widow for nearly 50 years. She never ailed the whole of her life; she never exercised, smoked 60 cigarettes per week and drank half a bottle of whisky a week. She was in perfect mental health and her favourite remark was that she had no tea to put in her whisky. A lifestyle to confound the experts.
John Wainwright, Wrose, Bradford

When I admired my elderly aunt's trendy, asymmetric new hairstyle, she retorted: "I'd rather be blue stocking than blue rinse."
Vera Roddam Renton, Woodthorpe, Nottingham

Older age is about slowing down and growing vertically, not

horizontally. That's not Ted. He has no belief in permanency and stability.
Jane Fonda on the end of her marriage to the tycoon Ted Turner

"It" girl Tamara Beckwith's father is asking his friends to take a timeshare in his apartment on a cruise liner. "As yet no one has expressed an interest," he says. "I think it's a wonderful idea but perhaps other people see it as a geriatric's sport."
Peter Beckwith

As a 75-year-old widower I confess to searching Rendezvous columns in *The Times* in the hope that one day I will strike lucky. However, I do find it off putting when the opposite sex stress "own hair and teeth essential". I would never dream of using anyone else's.
Alfred E. Norris, Point Clear, Essex

The only reason Patricia Hewitt, the minister for e-commerce, is not already in the Cabinet is that she left it rather late to be elected an MP – she was 48 when she entered the Commons in 1997.
The Daily Telegraph

My young dentist showed no surprise when I, aged 66, asked him to fit me with a sports mouthguard. Comfortably worn, this protects my own natural teeth and gives me confidence when playing younger, more agile, opponents in games that use hard balls.
Andrew Bell, Porthleven, Cornwall

Several years ago when I was 60, my daughter-in-law approached me with a view to my wife and I having one of her kittens. I demurred since we had recently lost our pet cat Puskas through feline cancer and his last moment had been particularly disturbing. "I don't want to go through that again," I said. To which she replied: "But you will have popped your clogs well before it does."
Mr W. T. Crawford, Alveston, Bristol

1 MAY 2001

I have an invalid husband and have a carer in for half an hour each morning to help. For the rest of the day and often during the night I take care of him myself. The DSS provides a carer's allowance for anyone who works 35 hours a week. It is a miserable £21 per week. Nevertheless, I applied for this allowance and was appalled to be informed that I am too old to qualify. It is paid only to people under the age of 65. I am 75. What possible difference could age make in this case?
Iris Craig, Bassett, Southampton

My husband has survived cancer twice and still plays tight-head prop every Saturday. In one match, they won by quite a margin against significantly younger opponents. My husband was one of a front row with a combined age of 150 years – he was 60, the hooker 51 and the other prop 49. Maybe a case of not dead yet . . . but who knows?
Linda Goldman, London, NW4

I recoil from the notion, now steadily gaining currency, that people in their sixties, seventies, eighties or thereafter should aspire to the romantic entanglements of those half their age.
Mary Kenny, The Sunday Telegraph

Extract from Sunderland FC supporters' song, sung to annoy Newcastle supporters, to the tune of Bobby Shaftoe: "Bobby Robson's 63/ In a hospice he should be."
Sheila FitzPatrick, Washington, Tyne and Wear

I have ordered a new Peugeot car but because I am now over 70, it will cost me £200 more. Why? I am now no longer eligible for the free car insurance package which comes with a new car, even though I have held a clean driving licence for more than 50 years and am fit with good eyesight. I think I am a

more careful driver than many youngsters who benefit from the "free" insurance package.
Dr Douglas C. Doughty, Tring, Hertfordshire

My indefatigable 72-year-old father, Doug, took his grandchildren to the Millennium Dome just before it closed. After eight hours of educational family fun, he returned the children, exhausted (them, not him). "He's amazing," commented William, aged 11. "Most grandpas sit in their chairs all day eating ham sandwiches."
Sarah Collett, Guildford, Surrey

8 MAY 2001

Tomorrow we announce the results of a MORI poll which illustrates how angry people are about the Government's refusal to pay for personal care. Our survey will have significant implications for candidates fighting marginal seats when voters will demonstrate their feelings at the ballot box. MPs who refuse to acknowledge their concerns do so at their peril.
Tessa Harding, head of policy at Help the Aged

At heart, I suspect she would like nothing better than to let go of the facelifts and dieting and settle down to blissful grannyhood.
The Julia Llewellyn Smith interview with Joan Rivers, Daily Express

The older body, like the older person, is quite as beautiful as the sleek young thing in magazines or on screen – more beautiful in some ways, with the added value of a mature character and experience.
Tom Kirkwood, The Reith Lectures

By the time I reach retirement age, the State will have had by far the greater part of everything I have earned. I will be too "well off" to qualify for support, and yet much too poor to live decently. Comparing my pittance with the amount spent on caring for burglars and TV licence dodgers, a series of custodial sentences might seem attractive as a means of respite, care and recuperation. Government had better build geriatric prison accommodation, or do something about the state pension we paid for.
George Edwards, Harrogate

I gave a talk on mathematics for three and four-year-olds to some NVQ mature students, and received a letter from the head of the school: "Thank you for your inspirational talk, the feedback has been very positive and the students are buzzing with excitement at seeing numbers and maths in a different light." I am 86 and had the common sense to take my husband along in case I forgot mid-sentence what I was about to say. He is a mere 84.
Dr Julia Matthews, Bexleyheath, Kent

A British Gas salesman, replacing a defective heating boiler, told me: "The makers will tell you this boiler will give 25 years' service." He looked up at me, hesitated, and continued: "But of course to you that would not be a selling point."
Kenneth J. Bruce (78) Watlington, Kings Lynn

I visited a new dentist for my six-monthly check-up. Having given me the all clear, he glanced at my notes, then remarked: "Those should see you out."
Mrs Angela Walder (72) Farnham, Surrey

15 MAY 2001

Following on from your Been There Done That column (May 8), I was one of the young mothers who organised the march by

women from Cardiff to Greenham in 1981. This resulted in the setting up of the Women's Peace Camp. To mark the anniversary we are taking part in another ten-day trek, across the Namibian desert in southern Africa during October, organised by the Mines Advisory Group (MAG). This British charity, which clears landmines and helps to rehabilitate victims, is a joint winner of the 1997 Nobel Peace Prize. If you are interested in joining the trek or sponsoring a trekker, tel: 0161-236 4311.
Karmen Thomas, Brynamman, Carmarthenshire

Some years ago I treated a vivacious lady of 95 who could have passed for at least 30 years younger. When I asked for the secret of her radiant health, she replied: "At last, I've managed to get my son into an old people's home."
Dr. E. Young (retired consultant), Reading

I had wanted for years to get Mrs Thatcher in front of my camera . . . as she got more powerful she got sort of sexier
Photographer Helmut Newton, 80

Retirement? You're talking about death, right?
Robert Altman, The Observer

Since I reached 80 there are several insurers who will not issue car insurance cover and others who quote very high premiums. I use glasses only for reading, and am fit enough to be the National Masters' Swimming champion. I coach swimming two days a week, do my own extensive gardening and DIY repairs – and sing in a choir. Yet those youngsters who man the telephones at call centres tell me I am too old to drive. I wonder how many of them could match me in a swim marathon?
Terry Jackson, Wike, Leeds

My mother Nancy is 83 and in her earlier days acted with all the great thespians – Dame Edith Evans was my godmother. She suffers from short-term memory loss and lives in a home

run by the cinema and television benevolent fund. But she still works. Recently she did a voiceover job in the West End, a modelling assignment, and last week she went to Copenhagen to shoot a commercial. She proves that with help from family, friends, carers, and, in my mother's case, her agent, an elderly lady who has trouble walking and lives in a home can still lead an active life.
Nigel Nevinson, Massongy, France

Even though the duo are both well into their forties, they haven't finished with pop music yet.
Article about the Pet Shop Boys in the London Evening Standard

22 MAY 2001

These days, you're not on your death-bed at 60. We've got to change society thinking that just because a bloke gets to 55 or 60 that he's automatically too old to do anything. That's not an old age these days.
Peter Thompson, new chairman of the National Association of Pension Funds in the Financial Times

I notice that in America people seem to be ageing much more rapidly. I don't know why; maybe they stop exercising, they eat too much sugar. I think it's a question of discipline.
Marcel Marceau, newly appointed spokesman for the World Assembly on Ageing

After commenting on the lack of a numerically appropriate card to give to my wife for our 42nd wedding anniversary, I remarked to the young woman shop assistant in the stationers that I would just have to add the words "plus two" to a ruby wedding card. "Fancy worrying about that," she said. "I'm surprised you're still able to count after being married that long. You're lucky you're still alive."
Ronald Hornsby, Burton upon Stather, North Lincolnshire

Source: York District Hospital reporting a PSA (Prostate Specific Antigen) result of 5.9 mg/ml (normal 0 to 4) to GP: An elevated PSA is not diagnostic of cancer of the prostate. If PSA is more than 4 mg/ml and the patient is less than 70 years of age, please consider urological referral.
Roger Partington, Upper Poppleton, York

I've always had a thing about older men. At school, during family visits, the girls would say "keep Arabella from Daddy", because I wasn't interested in the brothers, only the fathers.
Arabella Zamoyska, 27, recently married to Oliver Tobias, 53

29 MAY 2001

As if being 60 weren't bad enough, poor Bob Dylan has to face yet more re-appraisals of his life and work.
The Independent

If I'd known I was going to live as long as this, I would have taken care of myself.
Stanley Jones, 75, Northwood, Middlesex

Recently widowed, I decided to sell my house in Central London and look for a flat instead. An estate agent showed me one place with the "selling" point: "This would be ideal for your twilight years."
Mrs Margaret Coombes, 65, London NW1

If you need that extra little bit of motivation to keep fit and think young, you only need to see this recent photo of my mother, Pearl, practising her yoga. She was in her early 60s when she started going to yoga lessons and is 81 now.
Susan Leader, London

At breakfast with our two grandchildren, 10 and 7, they asked us why we took vitamin tablets. "To keep us young looking," my

husband replied. "Is it working?" They both looked hard at us and replied in unison, "No."
Molly Evans, Swansea

I was driving my father when the traffic lights changed from green to amber. I put my foot down and he said, "That's when you can tell you are getting older. To you, amber means go faster, to me it means slow down."
Stephanie Martin, Barnstaple, Devon

5 JUNE 2001

Police in Sun City West, Arizona, have logged more than two dozen complaints in a year of couples having sexual intercourse at swimming pools, car parks and on public benches. The average age of the perpetrators being 73.
London Evening Standard

The Roadhouse is good because the punters are right in your faces, just like they were in the Sixties when we started out in the clubs. It has kind of gone full circle for us guys.
Georgie Fame on playing with the Rhythm Kings

Not only are pensioners a very significant and growing section of British society, reflecting longer lifespans and smaller families, but the evidence shows that they register to vote and cast their ballots in greater proportions than younger people.
Dr Robert Waller, co-author of the Almanac of British Politics

Major George Llewellyn, repairing his trusty steed for the umpteenth time, told a press conference: "Retirement? Certainly not, merely another change of life. After stints as a soldier, businessman, work in the City of London and a furniture-maker, I am now engaged in photography, writing and bicycling – for fun and for charity." The major has raised an incredible £93,000 through sponsored pedalling to support our charity's work to prevent and cure blindness in some of the world's poorest communities.
Tabitha Cunniffe, Sight Savers International

William Hague had his best day of the campaign yesterday – all thanks to a couple of schoolgirl interviewers and a quayside of wrinklies.
Daily Mail

I'm about to get married again, so I'll have more kids. I have five already, the oldest is 26. Maybe I'll start a football team."
Stevie Wonder, 51

Last year my father fell against a wall and banged his head quite severely, which resulted in the formation of a haematoma. After several weeks of hospital care the consultant deemed him fit to be discharged. He reassured us that although the haematoma would eventually disappear, my father may suffer some degree of memory loss in later life. A

refreshing outlook on life expectancy, given that my father, now considerably recovered, is looking forward to his 95th birthday.
Mr C. M. Cordingley, Delph, Oldham

12 JUNE 2001

After a recent scripture lesson, my great-niece inquired, "Uncle, were you in the Ark?" When I replied somewhat indignantly, "Of course not," she asked, "Why weren't you drowned then?"
Martin R. Davies, Leigh Woods, Bristol

"You get older and suddenly you don't have to go out and do all that shit you do when you're young and dumb. Because now you're old and dumb instead."
Johnny Depp

On a visit to Drummond Castle Gardens, a wonderful topiary confection near Crieff, I was delighted to find that the concessionary admission for older people was listed not as "OAPs", nor even "senior citizens", but as "superadults". At the active age of 64, I like being classed as a "superadult". Others, please copy.
Antonia Bunch, Haddington, East Lothian

"I can only assume that it is largely due to the accumulation of toasts to my health over the years that I am still enjoying a fairly satisfactory state of health and have reached such an unexpectedly great age."
The Duke of Edinburgh, 80 on Sunday

Extract from the Parish Register of St Mary's, Haxby, York, for a burial in 1811: April 29 Elizabeth wife of John Moyser, died April 26 of old age – aged 58.
Jeremy Moiser, Glenfarg, Perthshire

Hurdling after a 40-year break in a veterans sports match for Oxford and Cambridge against Harvard and Yale, I limped in a painful second. Luckily the American universities travel with their own medical team and immediately their masseur checked the torn hamstring. He told me to lie down and breathe deeply while ice pads were applied. Then, apologetically, he said, "You know, sir, I don't think you should race again this week."

P. A. L. Vine, low hurdles champion 1955, 1956, Pulborough, Sussex

19 JUNE 2001

Many have wondered about her secret of longevity and I have to say it may have something to do with her lifetime love of Guinness.

Nick Murray, grandson of Amy Hulmes of Bury, who at 113 is officially the oldest woman in the world

While I was doing some supply teaching after retirement, a young boy of ten said to me: "You're old, aren't you?" (I was 64.) I made some suitable reply. He persisted – "Well 'ow old are yer?!" "Oh, I don't tell little boys how old I am," I replied. Rather a smug look came over his face, and thinking he was delivering the ultimate insult, he said: "You're 40, aren't yer?"

Margaret Hatcher, Berkhamstead, Hertfordshire

Recently I bought a new car. During the sales talk I mentioned that I had bought my first car in 1954. "Good Heavens!" said the salesman. "There can't have been many women drivers in those days." (I am still in my sixties.)

Maureen Threlfall, Preston, Lancashire

When a woman gets to her middle years, when she's really getting it together about who she is, is that the moment to consign her to the scrapheap? That would be like taking down a wonderful old building and replacing it with steel and chrome

and glass. Its lines might be sleek and perfect, but where's the
character?
Linda Gray (Sue Ellen in Dallas*) now 60. You magazine, The Mail on*
Sunday

"I couldn't get her off so I got on my knees and sank my teeth
into her neck."
Margaret Hargrove, 73, from Tallahassee, Florida, who saved her
Scottish terrier's life by biting the pit bull terrier that was attacking it,
The Mirror

I wouldn't mind someone old, as long as he could make me
laugh – though I've not yet reached the stage where I'd agree
that liniment oil is a decent replacement for sex.
Stephanie Beacham, actress, "fifties"

Sometimes I feel 95.
Kym Marsh, 25, of the pop group Hear'Say, who partly attributes her
fatigue to things "like smiling all the time".
Sunday Times Magazine

26 JUNE 2001

The former racing driver Allan Stuart-Hutcheson, 68, is to
marry for the sixth time. His bride-to-be is a 26-year-old half
Vietnamese woman. "I would appreciate it if you didn't mention

my first four wives – they are as worn out as the subject," he said.
Nigel Dempster, Daily Mail

You have to admit that Maureen Lipman is a game girl. At an age when she could be forgiven for doing nothing more challenging than mulching her Muswell Hill flowerbeds . . .
Maureen Paton on the actress's appearance in in the Vagina Monologues

When working in Iran I was introduced to the Imam of an important mosque who invited me to guess his age, which could not have been less than 80. "Sixty," I replied, evoking approving smiles all round. "And how old do you think I am?" I asked. "75," came the quavering reply. I was 50. So much for diplomacy.
Leslie Collier, London NW1

Carmen dell'Orifice, at 70 the oldest supermodel in the world, throws back her head and laughs. But then, keeping your chin up takes on a whole new meaning when you've got incipient jowliness to worry about.
Edward Helmore, London Evening Standard

My mother is 96, and had a bad fall and a blackout a few days ago. The doctor who examined her in the A&E clearly thought she was a bit gaga, so asked her to count down from 20. "Better than that," she said, "I'll do it in French," and got down to "douze" before the doctor said "OK, OK." She then said: "I like to show off now and again." The doctor was somewhat chastened.
David Horchover, Pinner, Middlesex

Mark Ravenhill, whose first play *Shopping and F** caused outrage, plans to stage his latest work at the National Theatre. It is called *Mother Clap's Milly House*, a period comedy

featuring graphic depictions of gay sex. "I haven't come up with a suitable play my mother can go to see," he admitted.
Sunday Times

10 JULY 2001

Sophia Loren, despite her age, was recently voted the most beautiful women in the world.
The Independent

Ken Clarke will be an old-age pensioner by the next election.
The Daily Telegraph

Support for medical research into illnesses affecting people in old age is not viewed as a priority by the general public. People across the UK were asked to name the two or three forms of medical research most deserving of additional financial support. Cancer came top (81 per cent) followed by heart disease (52 per cent) and children's illnesses such as asthma and leukemia (50 per cent). Only 20 per cent said that research into illnesses such as arthritis or dementia, should be given more funding.
Help the Aged

I take quite a series of vitamins, maybe 15 or so every day. I can act until I'm 103. I can find some toothless guy that's needed. I'll fall down the stairs as a toothless guy. I'll be good when I'm old."
Jon Voight, 63

In the Lakota native American language there is no word for "child". They are called "sacred beings" between the ages of 0–11 years. After that, everyone is a "youth" from 12–45. But best of all, for the rest of their lives a person is then either a "real man" or a "real woman".
Margaret Harrison, Leicester

Recently I visited Alabama Old Town, a collection of buildings in Montgomery, America, which are kept as they were when the Civil War broke out. It was swarming with schoolchildren. One of the youngest – I imagine just starting primary school – looked hard at me and asked: "Do you remember the Civil War?"
Emeritus Professor M. Hammerton, Department of Psychology, University of Newcastle

I have to admit I am not as young as I was and I'm not much of a walker now, but I don't have to walk on the sea. In a boat I lose 20 or 30 years straight away.
Helen Tew, 89, after her epic trans-Atlantic voyage

When you are over 50 it depends what day it is whether you can do a number of things.
Former President Bill Clinton

17 JULY 2001

In the new edition of *Collins Cobuild English Dictionary, for Advanced Learners* the following entry appears under "feisty": "If you describe someone as 'feisty', you mean that they are tough, independent, and spirited, often when you would not expect them to be, for example because they are old or ill: at 66, she was as feisty as ever."
Margorie Fisher, Stratford-upon-Avon, Warwickshire

In two years time I will be 50. But age doesn't hold any terrors for me because I feel stronger than ever. You stand there in the middle of your life and look backwards and forwards and give thanks for all the blessings you have had.
Pierce Brosnan

Life expectancy for men in England and Wales has risen from 69 to 74 in the past two decades.
The Office for National Statistics

Yves Saint Laurent shows why, at the age of 65, he is still unassailable.
The Daily Telegraph

During the recent Census I delivered a form to a gentleman who asked for help in completing it. Afterwards he said "Thank you, I'll know better next time." He was 92.
Sidney French (only 63), Canterbury.

On returning from a fabulous hotel holiday my 91-year-old mother decided to re-book and repeat the pleasures along with her, rather junior, 81-year-old pal. Careful to protect my inheritance she told me, "If I snuff it beforehand all you'll lose is the deposit."
Geoff Dossetter, West Malling, Kent

When my wife and I asked a young pharmacist for advice on the daily amount of salt we should be taking, he asked how old we were. We told him 75. He replied: "At 75 I wouldn't care how much I took."
W. H. Cousins, Upminster, Essex

Middle-aged dudes rule, OK? I see nothing wrong with 40, 50 or 60 year-old men dressing and acting like teenagers. I'm an elderly man of 44 and, after a few miserable years of being sensible, I do it all the time.
Jeremy Clarkson, The Sunday Times

Don't do it, guys. Please don't try to be hip past the age of 40. It doesn't work. There are enough ageing females struggling to retain that glimmer of youth.
Daily Mail

24 JULY 2001

I like working with young people. I decided long ago never to reveal my true age – it influences others' perception of you.
Carmen Silvera

Traditionally watched by old buffers in blazers and bacon-and-egg ties, cricket is going into overdrive to sell itself to a new generation of fans.
London Evening Standard

On reaching my 60th birthday, I decided that for the rest of my life I would be on holiday and just work as a spare-time hobby. It is called "reframing the problem".
Leonard Gibbons, Hull

There was no shortage of glamorous female leads, even if they were a little on the mature side.
Press Association report on the Archer trial

Putting us old sitcom actors together with an enthusiastic young crew is brilliant, even though half of them thought we were long dead.
Melvyn Hayes, in the new BBC series Revolver

My 92-year-old aunt, in hospital to have a pacemaker fitted, was asked by the nurse preparing her for the operation: "Please give me your teeth." "Certainly not," was her stern reply. She still has her own.
Roger Lines, Langport, Somerset

I remember my first ballet class when I was five, the day I won a beauty contest at 17, and the day I first discussed menopause symptoms with my doctor. But I finally realised I was getting old when I began to think that clothes simply serve a utilitarian purpose.
Christine M. Moulie, London NW1

31 JULY 2001

Discussing the forthcoming contest to fill the gap that will be left on the *Today* programme when Sue McGregor steps down as a presenter, the Editor Rod Liddle commented: "It would be nice to have a few people under 40 with a bit of edge to them."
New Statesman

When I was in my early sixties a friend referred to me as "old". "Only someone at least 15 years older than I am can be called 'old'," I said. Over the years this has been reduced to ten years. As I am now in my ninth decade by how much should I now reduce the gap?
Mrs Hilary Kay, Shirehampton, Bristol

My uncle and aunt, aged respectively 89 and 87, came from Paris to do some shopping in London. My uncle tried on a cardigan and asked my aunt for advice. "This is not for you, it's for an old man," she said. A happy couple who have been married for more than 60 years.
Lady Lipworth, London NW8

The sight of an old woman (Joan Collins) still apparently believing that self-esteem depends on looking good and having a man is profoundly depressing, not to mention exhausting.
Frances Taylor, The Sunday Times

Teaching is a busy process. Often during a lesson a pupil will put up their hand and inadvertently say "dad" or even "mum", but I was really depressed in a recent lesson when a similar event happened only this time the student said "grandad".
Robin Aung, 55, Cheddar

I can't wait until I'm 30 and I give up modelling because I'll be wrinkly and my bottom will be sagging . . .
Jodie Kidd, Daily Mail

My 50th birthday coincided with a holiday to China. I learnt there that the Chinese think it ridiculous that anyone could be considered of age at 18 or 21. Rather, in China a person becomes of age when they are 50. They argue that there are still a few grey cells working and, coupled with some experiences of life – marriage, family, work etc – a person is now about ready to comment and be listened to. How sensible. I was cheered up no end.
John D. Quigley, Weston, Cheshire

7 AUGUST 2001

Carmen dell'Orifice is not the world's oldest working model. My friend Pam Phillips is 71 and is getting more modelling work than ever. You name it, she does it – even dancing with the Pet Shop Boys on television. Like me she believes in ageing naturally, with no silicone, no plastic surgery, no hair colouring, no HRT. Nothing except good food and good sex.
Erica Adams, Tunbridge Wells

My 84-year-old mother still plays competition bowls. During a

match in the recent hot spell she fainted. After coming round and drinking a glass of water she insisted on continuing the game – which she won. Father, 86, said: "You could have died." "And what a wonderful way to go," was her reply.
Christina Page, Shrewsbury

My father saw the music hall star Marie Lloyd in 1922. I was thrilled when I saw that the Fortune Theatre was putting on a show about her life, starring Elizabeth Mansfield. I wrote to the theatre telling them about my Dad and that I would be bringing him to see the show on his 90th birthday. The theatre had left a card for Dad at the box office. It said: "Happy Birthday. Meet me at the stage door after the show. Elizabeth Mansfield." We did, and Dad was thrilled to get a birthday kiss from "Marie Lloyd". When Mansfield asked him how she compared with the original, Dad gave her a glowing review, although he did remark that Lloyd always had an orchestra; not just the piano accompanist that Mansfield had. "Still, you probably can't afford a full orchestra, like she could." he said. (Marie Lloyd was the Madonna of her day.)
Maggie Owen, Boulder, Colorado, USA

Motor racing is no longer a sport (referring to the tendency of drivers to ram rivals). It is just a business and the camaraderie has gone. I am sure that the chaps today would have behaved like us if they had been racing 40 years ago. But I hate to think if we were around today that we would behave like them.
Stirling Moss, 71

I was 20 and in the Royal Army Medical Corps when taken prisoner by the Japanese. I wasn't a doctor but had to perform amputations with a rusty knife. We mushed rotten bananas and spat into the resulting gunge. With the yeast that developed, vitamin B deficiency could be prevented. When I came out, the Government gave me £210 back pay but docked me 1s 6d (71/2p) for breaking a thermometer. I am now 80. Being old and healthy is wonderful.
George Holland, Aberdeen

14 AUGUST 2001

According to *USA Today*, baby boomers in America are the biggest buyers of skimpy beachwear. To illustrate the claim, they published a picture of a retired police officer from Virginia, 52-year-old Maralyn Herschey, wearing an orange bikini, who is quoted as saying: "I'm not dead yet." The law officer also thinks *Playboy* should start a new slot called middle-aged spread.
Frankie McGowan, on holiday in San Francisco

I was watching television one evening with my wife and mother, aged 90, when a rather risqué scene appeared. My wife, a little embarrassed, wanted to change channels but my mother stopped her by saying: "Don't do that. We might learn something!"
George Jamieson, Radcliffe on Trent, Notts

I had my first son when I was 18. I was young and stupid and I

grew up with the children. Having a son now, when I'm older and established, means that I can wallow in the parenthood thing. I'd highly recommend it to anyone really.
Paul Hogan (Crocodile Dundee) at 60, Mail on Sunday

I'm coming up to 67, fit, still working, and until recently felt no different than I did when I was 15 years younger. However, I am coming to the conclusion that I am being slowly conditioned to feel my age. For example, as soon as you reach 65, private medical insurance is automatically increased. Yesterday I did not get a quotation for car hire off the internet because the online system would not quote for anyone over 65 (or under 18). The same applies to holiday medical cover, which doubles if you do not lie about your age. No wonder I feel undermined.
Roy Clark (e-mail)

On his Radio 2 *Breakfast Show* Terry Wogan says: "I feel like an old geezer!" Then a pause and that characteristic wry chuckle: "Well, I am an old geezer." Indeed he is. Wogan has just turned 63.
David Thomas, Sunday Telegraph

21 AUGUST 2001

With Elton John still a firm fan, the jeweller Theo Fennell proves he has lost none of his sparkle at the age of 50, says Lydia Slater.
The Sunday Times

I needed to sign a document and the bank clerk offered me a pen. On completion, he remarked on the fact that my hand did not shake. At the time I was preparing to contest my seventh Parliamentary election. (I have lost my deposit at all of them.)
Robert Goodall, 85, West Derby

I shall be 70 in two months' time and feel exactly as I did when I was 20. I was idle and indolent then, and little has changed in the past 50 years except that perhaps now I am better at getting away with it.
Arnold Thomson, Gerrards Cross, Buckinghamshire

I am a Mystery Shopper visiting shops, pubs, banks, garages, etc. However, now I have turned 50, I have been told that I am too old to visit and eat at a pizza restaurant chain I used to assess. Despite my "advanced" years I still like pizza. I know others in my age-group who do too. We are the ones with the money to eat out and do so quite often. In fact, my elderly teeth are far less likely to fall out eating a pizza than struggling on a steak.
Zena Nattriss, Reading

At her recent birthday party my grandmother, 92, was scornful of one of her presents. It was a beautiful walking stick. Her only comment was, "They are trying to make me into an old woman."
Louise Hallam, Tunbridge Wells

I have always considered that anybody ten years older than me is middle-aged and that there is no such stage which can be labelled as old age.
Viscount Simon, House of Lords

Always marry a guy who's like, 55 years older than you. So everyone says "Isn't it shocking! A beautiful young woman of 65 marrying a 130-year-old man!" More importantly, always make yourself older, so everyone says "Seventy-seven? She's spectacular! Her arm is the arm of a 45-year-old." Just lie older. Very California!
Designer Michael Kors

Millie is a skilled sequence dancer. It was, therefore, surprising to see her at a beginners' class. Her reason? She wanted to pick up some teaching tips to help her with the class she runs for "the old folk". Millie will be 82 next birthday.
Marie Fairbairn, Cumbria

Plantsman in Burston's Garden Centre to 60-plus tree-buyer: "I wouldn't choose that one – it's a slow grower."
S. Russell, Watford

28 AUGUST 2001

Paula Rego is now 66. She is on the cusp of proper old age. Ahead of her are the years of terminality. And were she really one of ours, we would expect her to begin taking the weight off her feet round about now, to sink back in her armchair and embark on an inner life of rumination and yearning, regret and silence. Her anger ought to be turning into melancholy. And sex – one of her favourite motor forces – ought to be becoming a memory rather than a growing hazard.
Waldemar Januszczak, The Sunday Times. Sent in by Kate Taylor, 68, Wakefield

If I were starting now, I don't think I would be good-looking enough. There's much less room now for normal-looking people, which I think is a sad thing.
Victoria Wood

At 75, I have been appointed director-general of Professor Gaffar Medical Centre for Liver Diseases and Research, Cairo. Certainly the hospital board was looking for quality, and not for age or beauty.
Mahmoud Kay Booz, FRCS Bristol

Seen recently on the back of a battered-looking camper van in Thurlton, Norfolk: Old Age Travellers.
Jenny Rogers, Reedham, Norfolk

We should stop thinking of older people as problems and acknowledge that most of them have solved more problems than we've had hot breakfasts. The quality of my later life should be mainly up to me and I should prepare myself for the psychological as well as the possible pitfalls that will appear in the road before me. Others can help from time to time by clearing the road of unnecessary obstacles to my continued good health and financial well-being, but some of the obstacles to mental health and emotional well-being only I can deal with.
From a speech Richard Holloway, former bishop of Edinburgh, made at a conference held by the British Society of Gerontology

4 SEPTEMBER 2001

The older I get, the more it suits me. I think I was just waiting to grow older so I could sing and write songs that had more substance to them.
Nick Lowe, one of whose songs was used on the soundtrack of The Bodyguard

Arriving home from school after his first history lesson, my son asked: "Mummy, did you like it when Julius Caesar was here?"
Mrs Marjorie Kirwan, Chatham, Kent

At my 70th birthday bash Lorraine Heggessey, the Controller of BBC1, read out a poem she had written about me. One of the verses was about *Animal Hospital* and the risk that she had taken in choosing me as its presenter instead of a bright young thing. Her boss, Alan Yentob, told her afterwards that if she had been wrong she would have lost her job.
Rolf Harris

A few days ago my wife celebrated her 77th birthday. I bought her a new bicycle.
Tim Hardy, Hove

I am old enough that I'm thinking about being older.
Sean Penn

I am a rugby referee in my seventies. Last season my first match was at a new club which was using school premises for the first time. On arrival I went to inspect the pitch, at which point the home captain greeted me with: "Hello, you must be the caretaker."
R. G. Campbell, Chesterfield

11 SEPTEMBER 2001

Dying doesn't frighten me in the slightest though I should love to see my grandchildren grow up, but I don't want to get old and infirm and not be able to enjoy my life."
Beryl Bainbridge

I am 39 and have just completed the Snowdon International Race, an impossibly hard ten-mile run. Being well-pleased with my finishing time of 1 hr 45 min, I walked back to my car and struck up a conversation with a fellow competitor.

"How did you get on? I inquired. "Oh, not too good, 1hr 40min, my worst time yet. Still there is always next year." He was 68.
Peter Warner, Napton, Rugby

Now that I am in my seventies, I keep telling my wife what an advantage it is for her to be married to a palaeontologist: the older she gets, the more I love her.
Stuart Baldwin, Witham, Essex

Customers of all ages and sex dribbled in for their cut and blow dry, gentlemen arriving for their Saturday morning brush-up, children and pensioners coming in to be made more human.
Tracey Allen in Limited Edition, a local magazine, sent in by Peter Shears of Lewes

Mick Jagger's mouthpiece told *Hello!* magazine: "We are horrified that *Saga* put Mick on the front cover."

Me to my great-grandson, 9: "I wish I could preserve your smile." Great-grandson to me: "I wish I could bottle your laughter."
Celia Kennard, Harrow, Middlesex

18 SEPTEMBER 2001

I am playing grandmothers in movies now. I'd like to be one for real but my kids are not co-operating with me. Every time I have a birthday, every disc jockey in Hollywood starts yahooing it all over the place. But if you can't have fun as an ageing sex symbol when you hit 60, I don't know what will become of you.
Raquel Welch

Last week, my mother telephoned her internet service provider

to resolve a technical problem with her e-mail. To confirm her identity she was asked several questions, including her date of birth. The young man at the other end of the line paused, then twice asked her to repeat it. Finally he said, "What do you mean, 1914? Do you honestly mean to say you're, um, 87 years old?" When my mother laughingly confirmed the point, the young man replied, "Wow. I had no idea anyone that old used the internet".
Susan Bovee, Virginia, USA

Discussing a possible revival of the Seventies rock show *The Old Grey Whistle Test* (OGWT), producer Mike Appleton explained the origins of the name: "In the days of Tin Pan Alley, they would take the first pressings of a record and play it to the people they called the 'Old Greys' – the doormen, the delivery men – and if they could whistle the melody, they had a hit song."
The Daily Telegraph

If they brought back OGWT I expect they'd aim it at 33 to 55-year-olds. And I'm 55, so they'd think "oh, Bob Harris is too old".
"Whispering" Bob Harris, former OGWT presenter

In this country ageism is institutionalised. At 65, regardless of your physical or mental fitness, your holiday insurance premium is likely to be double what it was the day before. At 70, again regardless of fitness, you have to obtain a new driving licence and renew it every three years at £6 a time. Of all NHS patients, only pensioners must contribute to their care after six weeks in hospital. They then lose some of their state pension, even though the pension is based on insurance premiums.

W. H. Cousins, Upminster, Essex

There aren't many actors of his (Michael Caine's) vintage who are playing parts which suggest that the life force is still very much intact, without humiliating themselves by agreeing to be presented as romantic leads for actresses half their age.

The Times Magazine

25 SEPTEMBER 2001

Playing in the ladies singles tournament at my local tennis club last month, I was pleased to win a match against a lady of 30. With both of us admitting that we were not as fit as we would wish, my opponent remarked: "But you are so sprightly." Sprightly! I am only 54 years old.

Dorrie Manders, Alcester, Warwickshire

Elle Macpherson has just come back from two months in Ibiza . . . the break seems to have paid off because, even at 37, Elle looks very, very lovely.

Simon Mills, the Evening Standard

It is only when you are at childbearing age that physical appearance is important. Once you are beyond procreation, you relate more as human beings. The male/female pairing off goes on, but it is more spiritual – less to do with lust and more to do with love, which is not a bad thing.

Fay Weldon

Mary Wesley has thick white hair, endless legs and the captivating face that made her such a sexy beauty in her youth. Next year she will be 90, which she finds rather irritating because there is nothing elderly about her.
Lynda Lee-Potter, Daily Mail

This year I wasn't going to be able to make the Ryder Cup but I was looking forward to watching it on the box. That's all I can do these days. I've just had to accept that, at 87, my golfing days are over. I'm totally past it. But I've had a good innings, if you can call it that.
Sir Denis Thatcher, The Daily Telegraph

Three senior officials in the New York Fire Department who died at the World Trade Centre were aged 54, 63 and 71 respectively (*Times* obituaries September 14) and an architect who survived was aged 70 (*Times* same date). Does the USA value experience and expertise more than we do?
Anthony J. Roberts, Shoreham, Sussex

This week John Peel is on four networks and celebrates 40 years on air. Try getting your head round that.
Liz Kershaw, The Independent

2 OCTOBER 2001

My daughter's sixth form group were asked to discuss problems that older people might have. The tutor asked what problems they thought a 50-year-old person would encounter. One student replied: "I think they would have difficulty dressing themselves." My daughter was delighted to relay this to me.
Margaret Mattingley, Hindhead, Surrey

Does he understand how some find it unpalatable that an elderly man (Woody Allen is 65) should cast himself opposite far younger women? He does not. "It's a factor seized upon by

people who don't like me, who are reaching for something to say and they find that," he huffs. "There are many criticisms you could make of me, valid ones, but that I don't think is valid." He would, he insists, happily play opposite a 65-year-old woman should the story demand it.
Libby Brooks, The Guardian

The invite for *Top of the Pops* reads: "Over-18s but no wrinklies". Most of the audience weren't even born the last time David Cassidy was famous. Any older fans that do get into the studio will have their grey heads edited out of the broadcast.
Nick Curtis, Evening Standard

For the first time this year I have felt older. I've felt I'm slowly becoming more decrepit. It's when physical things happen. When you try and run 100 yards and find out you're not fit any more. I think you just move into the country and wear an old fleece.
Jennifer Saunders, 43

On BBC Radio 4's *Today* programme the discussion was the possibility of germ warfare and its terrifying consequences. James Naughtie said, "Of course, there are few people around today who remember the last war."
B. Brereton, Lancashire

Five years ago, Brendan Gleeson found himself outside the offices of a prominent Hollywood agent. "He said I was too old and too ugly," Gleeson remembers with a shudder.
The Independent

9 OCTOBER 2001

The prospect of stripping off in front of an audience would send most 60-year-old women running for cover.
Daily Mail, *commenting on Linda Gray currently playing Mrs Robinson in The Graduate*

I never think one whit about age. I think it's the most boring subject in the world. How you look has everything to do with the attitude you've got. I know people in their 30s who have old attitudes. The older I've got, the more free I've felt. And I'm certainly not going to start lying about my age.
Linda Gray, 61

I'd like to write something for my own pleasure and satisfaction before I lapse into final senility. I don't care if it's published or not; I'll put it under the stairs and my great-grandchildren can do what they like with it.
Jan Morris

You must all have had trouble getting a literate secretary who knows where to put the commas and full stops. With anyone under the age of 45, it is almost impossible.
Professor Graham Zellick

Having always hated the elitist, certain-age competitiveness of Western aerobics, to see people of every shape and age all exercising together is uplifting.
Francesca Annis in Good Housekeeping, describing a visit to China on her own

Men in their forties and fifties are a lost generation, caught between the confidence of their fathers and the liberalism of their sons.
Monica Troughton, Daily Mail

I'm developing a new fondness for Michael Douglas, now that he's getting all menopausal and wrinkly.
John Patterson, The Guardian

16 OCTOBER 2001

I know it's the male menopause but I fancy a 500cc Kawasaki.
Sir Paul Nurse on how he proposes to spend his share of the £680,000 Nobel Prize for Medicine

Recently I took an elderly neighbour to the cinema. As we went to buy tickets, the young man inquired brightly: "Any concessions?" Drawing herself to her full 4ft 11in, my 93-year-old friend said coyly: "Well, I am a pensioner." He replied sweetly: "I never presume – it can give offence."
Carol Reid, Brighton

All my life I have sneered at the old farts who said that the world is going to the dogs, and at last I have realised, my God, they are right.
Jan Morris

My mother (a doctor, who graduated nearly a century ago) used to say that the seven ages were: childhood, adolescence, adulthood, middle-age, elderly, old and wonderful. She died, aged 97, still able to have a stab at *The Times* crossword. Definitely wonderful.
Mrs Mary Wilson, Somerton, Somerset

I know a lady who is looking for voluntary work. She says: "I have plenty of spare time, I have all my faculties and I would love to do something that will help other people. But it must be something I can do sitting down." She is 90.
Brenda Arnell, Cranleigh, Surrey

The final verse of my poem on growing older reads:
> So when you see my wrinkled face
> And insist I take your seat
> Don't think I'm churlish declining
> I'm just fighting to stay on my feet.

Dorothy Lamb, Ealing, London

23 OCTOBER 2001

The Times does a real service to 50-plussers with "not dead yet", but I fancy you scored an own goal with the front-page item on October 12 that was headed (no doubt by an

impossibly youthful sub-editor): "Grand old men of radio face
final sign-off". Ageism is rife in journalism and broadcasting,
but radio bravely withstands the onslaught because, generally,
voices do not decline in step with appearances. Jimmy Young,
78, and Alistair Cooke, 92, who were mentioned in the story as
being set up for the chop, Terry Wogan, Don Maclean, Bob
Harris, Ed Stewart and many others still deliver the goods and
should be allowed to continue to do so. They have personality,
style and experience, and I am sure that is good enough for
discerning listeners of all ages.
Brian West (a mere 66), Gwernymynydd, Flintshire

While driving my 101-year-old mother back to her nursing
home after our monthly picnic in the country, she remarked:
"You know, if anything happened to you I could not drive you
home." I am 71.
Christopher Catford, Ewhurst, Surrey

I started my three-year diploma course in nursing when I was
44. During my final months I was placed on the intensive care
unit at Leeds General Infirmary. The ICU consultant took one
look at me and said: "Good God, you must be the oldest
student in the world." Even now, two years later, I am not sure
whether to be amused or insulted.
Tony Clarey, Leeds

I was appalled to read on a packet of painkillers recently, "dose
for adults and the elderly". I have heard of a "second
childhood" but I didn't think it was that formalised. And when
does one cease being an adult in pharmacological terms?
Perhaps when one is given the tablet as opposed to helping
oneself?
Jessica Pacey, Newark, Nottinghamshire

"Old guys of 50-plus love me with a whip in my hand."
*Anne Robinson on Parkinson, October 13. Submitted by David Ray,
Rowton, Shropshire*

I am 56, and last weekend, while covered from head to toe in mud, during a cross-country mountain-bike ride, a fellow participant of similar age observed: "It is like being a naughty boy again, but we are too old for our mothers to complain."
Alan Thompson, Buxton

30 OCTOBER 2001

Julia Roberts now commands $20 million a movie, but the real question is not so much whether she is worth it, but why men are paid so much more. They don't have to be young – Harrison Ford gets $30 million and he is 58.
The Guardian

In a publicity coup for the Chiracs, Hillary Clinton appeared in a French television broadcast last week about Bernadette Chirac, the 68-year-old matron of the Elysée Palace.
The Sunday Times

Official Social Services-speak for the over 75s is: "Elderly elderly".
Stefan Ruff, Ogleforth, York

Backstage at the Milan fashion show Inès de la Fressange, 44, now a mother of two, was being feted for returning to modelling. "All anyone wanted to know was my age," she says. "I told them I was 50, because it's so much more glamorous to look younger than your age, isn't it? And they all believed it. I was very shocked."

We run a B&B in Aldeburgh. Recently a lady in her eighties booked accommodation for her son and his wife, both in their sixties. "Could you give us some idea what time they will arrive?" we asked, to which we received the reply: "Oh, good heavens no. You know what these young things are like."
John and Linda Connah

I had something to prove, not so much to anyone else as to myself. I was resolved to show that, even at 54, I could still become the first to complete a voyage that no man had accomplished before. This is why I rowed across the Pacific Ocean.
From Bold Man of the Sea by Jim Shekhdar

On seeing my photograph on my credit card, the young chap accepting it at a petrol station said: "This wouldn't be much use to a young bloke if he nicked it."
Dick Comyn, 67, Cavendish, Suffolk

Everyone says I am terrified of getting old but the truth is that in my job becoming old and becoming extinct are one and the same thing.
Cher

6 NOVEMBER 2001

Ageing gracefully is supposed to mean trying not to hide time passing and just looking a wreck. That's what they call ageing gracefully. You know? Don't worry girls, look like a wreck, that's the way it goes. You suffer when you give birth, it doesn't matter, it's nature, all that f* thing. Don't take care of yourself because you want to stop time, do it for self-respect. It's an incredible gift, the energy of life. You don't have to be a wreck. One's aim in life should be to die in good health.
Jeanne Moreau

If you register with the electronic *Daily Telegraph*, you must give your date of birth; if you were born before January 1, 1920, you have to lie, as this is the earliest you are allowed to have been born. Obviously the paper deems everyone over 81 either not worth bothering about or incapable of surfing the Net.
Stephanie Jenkins, Headington, Oxford

As a responsible grandfather, Tony Booth has given up drink and is now washed, pressed, trimmed and neat, like a pensioner on an outing.
Jane Kelly, Daily Mail

Jimmy Young's show, a mixture of current affairs and trivia, is regarded as twee by its critics, but increased its audience to 5.3 million in the last quarter. As Young gets even older . . .
Matt Wells, The Guardian

Using the internet, I booked a return flight with GO from Bristol to Nice. At the end of the booking procedure a new page appeared on the screen offering car hire. I keyed in my details, including my date of birth, only to receive the reply that there were no cars available. If there were no cars available, why was the offer made in the first place? I repeated the exercise, but lied about my age and indicated that I was 69. Sure enough, I could hire a car. Just to check, I submitted my details for a third time, using my correct age, and found that, as before, there were no cars available. Hertz was able to accommodate me with no fuss at my truthful age.
Ken Wilkins, Thornbury, Bristol

A kind of madness descends on men in their mid-to-late forties, and it's all to do with seeing your youth slipping over the hill. You yell "Hang on! Wait! I haven't finished with you." Isn't that sad?
Nicholas Evans, the author of The Horse Whisperer

13 NOVEMBER 2001

Robert Kilroy-Silk, I am told, is something of a heart-throb among those ladies of a certain age whose lives have become simplified into a stark choice between chores and chocolates.
Pete Clark, Evening Standard

When reporting on the Queen Mother's 100th birthday outside Clarence House, Jenny Bond had to climb up a 20ft ladder sans scanties – and told everyone so afterwards. She reminds me of those middle-aged sexpots who like to semaphore clumsy messages about their still smouldering libidos.
Jan Moir, The Daily Telegraph

Enjoying life is not an exclusive preserve of young people. It is far better to be out with beautiful girls than be an old fart in the pub talking about what you were like in the Sixties.
Mick Jagger on Channel 4

Greta Scacchi, at 41, still has the looks of a Hollywood star.
Ryan Gilbey, The Independent

On a recent train journey: I asked the ticket inspector if he would like to see my senior rail card, to which he replied: "No thank you, sir, that won't be necessary."
Emeritus Professor George Pratt, Starcross, Exeter

Having been around a while we now have more or less everything and if we want something, within reason, we can go out and buy it. Can your readers suggest a suitably imaginative Christmas present people like us can buy for their friends?
Joyce Newbold, Hemel Hempstead, Hertfordshire

What a crowd! Geriatric Guildford is out in full force for a rumbustious comedy in which Joan Collins plays a glamorous old trouper.
Ginny Dougary, The Times Magazine, from Julian Corlett, Scunthorpe

The entry on William Shield (1748–1829) in *The New Grove Dictionary of Music and Musicians* says of him: "In old age Shield produced two fascinating anthologies of music . . ." One of these was his *Introduction to Harmony* published in 1800, when he was 52.
John Valdimir Price, Cloudesley Square, Islington

20 NOVEMBER 2001

Although I'm 71, I'm just a big kid. Age is all an attitude. The attitude has got to be one of childlike wonder and joy at the amazing things there are in the world. Inside, I feel absolutely marvellous. I think that you can pre-plan getting old by your attitude. You grow old when you start paying for your funeral in advance or taking out a pension when you're 30.
Rolf Harris, The Independent

His face was as weatherworn and furrowed as one might expect in a man of 58.
Robin Eggar on Mick Jagger in The Sunday Times

It does seem very peculiar to employ a pot-bellied, 62-year-old in a cardigan to champion sounds deliberately designed to make most parents' toes curl.
Matthew Bannister on John Peel in The Times's Play section

From an Aids information leaflet picked up at the border of Botswana and Namibia. ". . . sexually active people (defined as between the ages of 19 and 49)"
Simon Fernley, Bath

Lace isn't just for grannies.
The Guardian

I have married a man 35 years younger than myself. A day or two before our wedding in Las Vegas, we saw some gas balloons for sale. One said: "If older is better, then you're approaching magnificent." My husband-to-be thought it was a great decoration for our wedding.
Dorienne Board, Cipières, France

27 NOVEMBER 2001

I love swimming. Always have. I have been doing it since I was a child, so it feels as natural to me as walking. And when you get as old as I am, you find that you can swim a lot better than you can walk.
Oliver Sacks, 68, the American neurologist and author of The Man Who Mistook His Wife for a Hat in the Telegraph magazine

Responding to the invitation to "Apply now" for student support in my local paper, I rang Wandsworth Borough Council. I told the official that I had been offered a place on a postgraduate course at London University and would like to know how to proceed. She informed me that 55 was as old as a student was allowed to be to qualify. I commented that 55 was precisely the age when someone retiring from a regular job might want to go back to school. She said it was not the local authority but the Government that decided these things.
Diana Coke, 65, London SW15

At Salisbury Magistrates' Court, Margaret Phelps, 61, pleaded guilty to harassing David Conio, a 62-year-old removal man. She sent him love letters, bottles of whisky and played Elvis Presley's *Love Me Tender* down the phone. After Phelps was given a 12-month community rehabilitation order and a 12 month restraining order, Mr Conio commented: "You expect that sort of behaviour from a young, besotted teenager who has been turned down in the love stakes, but not by a 61-year-old woman."
The Times

"Considering that Percy Grainger was pushing 70 when he penned this piece (*Seventeen come Sunday*) it shows that the old man had not lost any of his faculties." David Mellor on Classic FM.
Dr Peter Lewis, Tenterden, Kent

Jim Davidson lives in Oliver Reed's old place, down in Surrey between Dorking and Horsham. He welcomes me at the door – a good-looking man, blue eyes, red-blond hair, fit for almost 48.
Robert Crampton, The Times Magazine

4 DECEMBER 2001

Anita Pallenberg is everywhere. What is more, Anita Style – wearing masculine clothes in a feminine way – is going strong for 2002. "I guess the girls like it because it's really casual." Pallenberg grins her signature bad-girl grin, still intact though she's 55 and a grandmother.
Shane Watson, Evening Standard

I wanted to boost our school kitty so I invited brothers and sisters, babies, granny and granddad, even pets, to join the annual school photograph day. The granddads looked splendid with hair slicked into place, in best suits and teeth.
Mike Sullivan, education consultant, The TES

There are some tensions between the generally more svelte younger players on the professional women's tour and their more solidly built elders. Earlier this month Norway's Suzann Pettersen was furious at letting slip a last round lead at the German Open, but found consolation in that losing to a fellow glamorous youngster, Karine Icher, was not as bad as being beaten by an "old bag".
The Daily Telegraph

Crack open the Sanatogen, Jimmy Young has just signed a new, year-long contract with Radio 2.
Daily Mail

Recently in baking heat I struggled up a steep cobbled street. I am diabetic. One of our group admitted he was on Warfarin. A

lady who needed another hip replacement leaned on her stick
and remarked: "If I had died when I was 50, I would have died
healthy." We all laughed.
Sheila Bynner, Downham Market, Norfolk

Commenting on Cilla Black's appearance at the Royal Variety
Performance, Judy Cornwell, 59, said, "Marlene Dietrich used
to show a leg but I think showing everything once you are
approaching your sixties is dicey.

   And James Naughtie on the *Today* programme said of Cilla:
"She's no spring chicken."

11 DECEMBER 2001

Ant is wearing a denim jacket, while Dec sports a zip-up cardy.
"Don't call it a cardy," he wails, "it makes me sound really
middle-aged."
The Daily Telegraph

The music industry is praying for a break-even year with a
bonanza from its greatest-hits catalogues. A key reason why
music companies are dependent on artists of an earlier
generation, of course, stems from the failure of present-day

superstars to register a seismic presence. So far, music's superstar acts are like summer movies that open with a giant explosion but drop quickly.
Variety

When I first saw Theresa Russell, 44, she was bounding into the living room behind her retriever, Rusty, looking elastic as an adolescent.
Andrew Gumbel, The Independent

School-leavers in Germany are shying away from applying for many university courses normally regarded as the most popular, because of the large numbers of senior citizens filling the lecture theatres. They regard the presence of older students as "uncool".
Times Educational Supplement

Explaining why she was reluctant at first to date former Bond George Lazenby, 62, tennis star Pam Shriver, 39, says bluntly: "Age. I thought I should find someone within five years of my own age. But my history is older guys – I have a pretty strong personality and older guys can deal with it better."
Daily Mail

Adults will play the children's game Kerplunk!, long lost schoolfriends will be reunited to the music of Eighties pop idols, B-list celebrities will reminisce about adolescent kisses under mistletoe, and two lost episodes of *Dad's Army* will be aired. Jane Root, the BBC2 Controller, said she was trying to position the channel for an older audience.
The Times

Tipped to be one of the top pops this Christmas is *How Wonderful You Are* by Gordon Haskell. It is his first foray into the hit parade and he is 55. He got the idea for the song while waiting for his mother to choose her groceries in Safeway.
The Sun

18 DECEMBER 2001

Overheard on *Today*, BBC Radio 4, Sue McGregor interviewing someone from Bradford about the recent report into integrating communities: "Some of the people who come to this country are middle-aged or elderly and may not find it easy to learn a new language."
Jane Clayton, Loosley Row, Bucks

I represent a group of *Dad's Army* golfers aged 70 to 87 who play twice a week all year round. It is the regular practice for the youngest member to provide the port at our annual Christmas luncheon, which we look forward to in the next few days. We are not dead yet, although some of the older gentlemen have lost their drive.
Robert Grant (82), Dundee

Good news for all those guys in their 50s fearing professional termination – Arnold Schwarzenegger is coming back for a third outing as *The Terminator*.
Toby Moore in the Daily Express

Though it has been 20 years since Jeremy Irons, 53, set hearts racing as the moody star of *Brideshead Revisited* and *The French Lieutenant's Woman*, he can still be very convincing in the part of a romantic leading man.
Michael Shelden, The Daily Telegraph

I visited one of Yorkshire's great fish and chip restaurants where they were advertising a senior citizens special. I am 58 so assumed that this was not for me. Out of interest I asked what was their definition of a "senior citizen". The young waitress informed me that it applies to anyone over 45. I have been missing out for 13 years.
Dr Barrie Hopson, Adel, West Yorkshire

In *The Money Race*, the fourth novel of his Nick Shannon series, Paul Bennett describes someone: "He was pushing 50 – back from the wrong side; the sort of age when evenings are passed in contemplation of one's pension and spending it on coach tours of the bulb fields of Holland, a lifetime subscription to *The Oldie* and a bulk purchase of tartan slippers."
M. Coombes, Puddletown, Dorchester

2002

1 JANUARY 2002

From the *Evening Standard*: "But Riding's real problem is that, unlike her co-stars Jonathan Pryce and Dennis Waterman, she is primarily a creature of the theatre. At 34, her looks, frankly, get better the cheaper the seat you are in". Poor actress Joanna Riding! Only 34 and the reviewer Andrew Billen can't bear to sit close to her.
Saskia van der Linden, Brentford, Middlesex

At the Department of Psychology, University of Surrey we are conducting research on medical care at the final stages of life, and the degree to which older people would like to participate in the decision-making process. Adults aged 60 and over interested in participating should contact . . .
Advertisement in The Oldie submitted by Mike Buckley, Sawbridgeworth, Herts

I telephoned Saga, which advertises special rates for senior citizens, for a quote to insure my car. I received the highest quotation of any by some hundreds with the highest excess for my modest hatchback. When I protested they explained: "We don't expect our clients to have cars like that." The car is a

Seat Leon, 1.8 20V T, admittedly a smart performer but hardly
a Ferrari. Their quote was for £510. I settled with Norwich
Union for £329.
Raymond Moody, Burford Oxfordshire

"The best age for a man is 44," Kurt Vonnegut says. "When
you're 44, people finally take you seriously."
The Independent

Over the past four months, my company has trained more than
200 senior citizens in basic computer and internet skills. The
average age of trainees that have undertaken the specially
designed, hands-on course is 73. The oldest participant is 92.
Philip Birch, Sandwich, Kent

Like most older dads, Pete Postlethwaite struggles to keep up
with his children's fads and fancies.
Jan Moir, The Daily Telegraph

I was about to stand on a chair to change a light bulb when I
was stopped by the admonishing voice of my granddaughter,
Bryony. "Let *me* do that, Granny," she said. "I don't want you
falling and hurting yourself." I am 50, Bryony is 10.
Gillian Manning, Quedgeley, Gloucester

8 JANUARY 2002

Gordon Haskell's freakish hit *How Wonderful You Are*
comprises a dozen songs packed with fabricated world
weariness and tunes you're doomed to hear for ever in lifts and
drifting across supermarket aisles. Mostly the tone is wistful,
plaintive and sentimental, though occasionally Haskell clicks
up a notch into a kind of arthritic funk.
Adam Sweeting, The Guardian

Having attended computer classes for the past three years in an attempt to keep up with my children and grandchildren, I produced my personalised greetings cards using Microsoft Publisher with clipart images and feel pleased with my efforts as a 75-year-old. You can imagine my indignation when a cousin commented: "Your Christmas card is most original – did one of your grandchildren design it?"
Henry I. Parker, Alton, Stoke-on-Trent

At Liberty is the show that Elaine Stritch is bringing to Broadway for a ridiculously limited 80 performances. Why is she so lazy, doing just five performances a week? First, allow for the fact that it is a one-woman show, and being alone on stage for two-and-a-half hours can be tiring. Then you have to throw this into the mix: she is 76 years old.
William Goldman, Variety

Some years ago (I was 45 at the time) I was at the local library to renew my ticket. "You a pensioner?" asked the young man behind the desk. I told him I had another 15 years to go. "Oh sorry," he said, "I never can tell the difference between the old and the very old."
Margaret Spearman, Barnes, London SW13

"Frankly, this is starting to drive me nuts. I've been thinking about this for a long time. I'd like to be a father. But even if I get married and have a baby tomorrow, I'm going to be 57 when the kid is 20," laments Russell Crowe.
Evening Standard

I heard on the commentary on the Premiership on ITV, after a goal scored in the Leeds-Newcastle game: "Bobby Robson does a jig of delight on the touchline and then suddenly remembers he's 69."
Michael Henderson, Westward Ho, Devon

15 JANUARY 2002

I'm not a facelift person. For me, the trade-off is that something
of your soul goes away. You end up looking body-snatched.
That's just my view. It's not necessarily a popular view.
Robert Redford, The Times

Age has made me more respectful of mortality but not afraid. I
don't smoke any more and I only drink wine with meals. I'm a
great one for vitamins and exercise. My doctor tells me I'm in
very good nick. The most positive way to think about death is
to try to live.
Michael Caine, Daily Mail, Weekend

Recently, before boarding an aircraft at Gatwick, my wife had a
very small pair of nail scissors and a very small nailfile
confiscated from her cabin luggage on the ground that we
could be terrorists intending to use them to hijack the plane.
My wife is 86, I am 87.
Rex Darton, Surbiton, Surrey

The grey market is one of the real growth areas. You
absolutely cannot turn your back on several million people with
no responsibilities, great white spaces of discretionary time
and a lot of disposable cash.
Jeremy Bullmore, The Henley Centre

During a visit to China last month I visited the new city of
Shenzhen, where apparently only those under 30 can get an
initial residence permit. The city is filled with spectacular new
buildings and a cultural history park. At the latter I was
confronted by a notice next to the ticket office that
commanded: "The elderly of 60 years old and over and kids
should be accompanied." Nevertheless I did manage to
stagger round without assistance.
Andrew Parker, Reading

While she is by far the oldest member of the cast, Kim Cattrall has the looks and attitude to make the voraciously sensual, fortyish Samantha in *Sex and the City*, entirely believable. "I never thought I'd be playing this character at this age in my life," she says. "I thought I'd be playing somebody's mum."
John Hiscock, The Daily Telegraph

My lifetime's achievements all seemed less than memorable when, in my 77th year, my four-and-a-half-year-old grandson announced before our assembled families, "Grandpa, you are my hero."
Tony Watkins, Eastbourne

22 JANUARY 2002

An answer to the NHS waiting list: those of us over 75 years of age left school at 14 or 16 and have been paying into government funds before the NHS was even thought of. Wouldn't it be fairer to put those who have been paying longer at the front of the queue?
Walter Hope, Bury, Lancs

"It's a wet Sunday afternoon in Manhattan and many theatres are 'dark' or nearly empty after terrorist threats, so I assume there will be only a small audience for a pessimistic drama by an intellectual Swede starring two elderly English actors." – Andrew Duncan writing in the *Radio Times*. The "elderly" actors he is talking about are Helen Mirren and Ian McKellen.
Sylvia Mills, Sunningdale, Berkshire

Tina Brown, Editor of *Talk*, the American magazine that closed last week, said at the weekend: "I have no plans to retire and do my knitting." How patronising she sounds, and at least 30 years out of date. The last thing retired people have time to do is knit.
Helen Petrie (retired GP), Middlesborough

I am 72 and recently went for my annual flu jab. I was surprised to be offered one for pneumonia as well. Before accepting, I asked, among other questions, when I should need another. The nurse replied, brightly, "Oh, you won't. They last about ten years."
A. J. Wilkinson, Stockton-on-Tees

The equipment at the gym I attend includes several exercise bicycling machines with a control panel with the title "Life Fitness". The panel has the usual diagram showing, for a range of ages, the appropriate heart rate for exercise in the cardiac training zone or the fat-burning zone. The diagram goes no further than age 65. I hope to spend many years in their ghost zone.
David Perridge, London W13

Comparing the film *Black Hawk Down* with *Saving Private Ryan* and *Band of Brothers*, the panel on *Night Waves* on BBC Radio 3 agreed that comparison is limited because, while the incident portrayed in *Black Hawk Down* (starring Ewan McGregor) occurred within living memory (1993) the latter two are history (1945). One presumes they mean consigned to the dustbin thereof.
Christopher Macy, Wellingore, Lincoln

"I've got cheekier with age. You can get away with murder when you are 71 years old. People just think I'm a silly old fool. They know I'm lucky I am still standing."
Bernard Manning, The Daily Telegraph

29 JANUARY 2002

I feel so sorry for the Bridget Jones generation. They have more money, more choice, more freedom and yet still seem to be so unhappy and lost. They are more tired and have less sex. We had it every night when we first married.
Joanna Trollope, The Daily Telegraph

At a time when the BBC's *Blue Peter* is encouraging viewers to hold Bring & Buy sales to raise money for the elderly, this comment is of particular irony. During the show on Friday, January 18, advertising its latest competition to get viewers to meet their pop idols, the presenter said: "Please send in the name of your favourite pop star, and remember to include your age as we don't want a 59-year-old Tom Jones fan on the show."
Valerie Lodge, Bournemouth

I was "volunteered" by a step-grandchild to talk to his class of fellow six-year-olds about the toys I played with when I was a youngster. At question time I was asked whether my bicycle had a big wheel in front and a little wheel at the back. You try explaining to a group of six-year-olds the difference between being 76 and 176.
George Harris, Brixton, Plymouth

At the 14th World Veterans Track & Field Championships in Brisbane last July, 60-year-old Ester Linaker from Dunfermline recorded 14.26 seconds in her 100-metre heat of the Women's age group 60–64. At the IAAF World Athletics Championships in Edmonton in August, a 22-year-old male clocked 14.28 seconds in his heat of the 100 metres.
Bridget Cushen, Secretary, British Veterans Athletic Federation

If the diagrams on the equipment at David Perridge's gym (last week's Not Dead Yet) show an upper age limit of 65, he should come to mine in Newbury where there is a device marked in ten-year increments up to the age of 100. I think I'll stick with it. *Dum spiro, spero.*
Howard Paynter, Newbury

I must confess I'm getting a little bit fed up with the continual references to my age, although I suppose it is inevitable. I had plenty of bad games at 25 and I'll have plenty at 35. But that isn't because of my age, it's because I'm human.
Steve Claridge, Millwall striker, in the club's magazine

5 FEBRUARY 2002

Surveys to establish which women Americans most admire frequently place Oprah Winfrey first and Martha Stewart second (though her fans would take up their handsome-yet-practical Martha Stewart garden trowels to dispute that ranking). And at 60, the former model remains a sex symbol.
The Daily Telegraph

Professor Ezio Capizzano, 66, a commercial law lecturer at the University of Camerino, Italy, who is said to have given good grades to female students in return for sex, was hailed as a hero by Alberto Bevilacqua, a 68-year-old author of romantic novels. He said, "The professor stands to become the new guru of pensioned Italian males."
Corriere della Sera, Rome

The older I get, the more I learn. I'm coming to a whole new range of roles. I can now play grandfathers – Sir Derek Jacobi.
Daily Mail, Weekend

Iona Chatterton, aged 84, in conversation with her vicar about the idea of retiring to the country: "When you have one foot in the grave, you need the other on the pavement." Mrs Chatterton, widow of Bishop Chatterton, died four days short of her 105th birthday and was playing Scrabble with the wife of that same vicar, ten days before she died.
Canon John Oates, Rector of St Bride's, Fleet Street, 1984–2000

A businessman sent an elderly woman flying 20ft through the air when he landed his helicopter on the lawn of a hotel where she and her husband were having lunch. Jill Benham, 64 . . . .
Linus Gregoriadis, The Times

Our middle years ought to be a welcome period of calm and confidence, but many of us persist in behaving like teenagers until our mid-thirties (or later) and think being adult is, like, really uncool.
Geraldine Bedell, The Observer

Nor will I be alone in thinking that most women of Joanna Trollope's vintage and older, even if they were free to throw caution to the winds, just wouldn't be that interested in new romantic adventures.
Nicola Tyrer, Daily Mail

12 FEBRUARY 2002

When I look in the mirror I don't see a rock star any more. I see a little balding old guy who looks like someone's uncle.
   I'm comfortable with that.
Pete Townshend, 56, in The Sun

A platform speaker at a meeting in Edinburgh on euthanasia said: "I am not in favour of euthanasia but I am young. I don't know how I will feel when I am 50 or 60."
Dr Ian McKee, Edinburgh

I have a fabulous life – I work, I do beautiful shows (she sings for supper clubs and conventions), I have a tremendous gang of friends and boyfriends. I hear women my age who talk about the difficulty of finding an escort. They advertise, they look on the internet. I have no problems at all.
Tonia Bern-Campbell, 65, in The Guardian

Norman Mailer may have come on stage at the Apollo Theatre last night professing deafness, leaning on two walking-sticks and in his 79th year, but the American writer proved he had lost none of his bite.
Evening Standard

My wife and I have just returned from our 30th successive annual ski-ing holiday. We skied down the Lauberhorn world cup course at Wengen to celebrate my wife's 69th birthday. When we returned home we found among the junk mail, a leaflet from Eagle Star Insurance offering special rates to over-60s. Eagle Star seems to think that the only sport we are capable of participating in at our age is bowls, as the leaflet was in the shape of a bowls wood.
Tony Bromley, Ringwood, Hants

With Sondheim and Rodgers & Hammerstein now becoming oh-so-20th century, old rock stars – Roger Taylor, Brian May and Bruce Springsteen – are queuing up to create stage shows from their music."
The Daily Telegraph

A woman aged 53 battled for 12 hours through snowdrifts and freezing winds to summon help for a climbing companion who had broken his ankles in an avalanche. Flight Sergeant Will

Hughes of the Rescue Co-ordination Centre at RAF Kinloss said: "This is a story of true grit. It is truly brilliant, a real epic. This woman really got both of them out of trouble. She is a definite heroine."
The Times

19 FEBRUARY 2002

I was in a shop and this good-looking young, trendy girl came up to me and said, "I really like your cardigan" and I thought, "yep, Karren, you've still got it". Then she said, "my mum would really like it". I thought: "What's happened to me? Old women want to know where I get my clothes. Where did it all go wrong?"
Karren Brady, managing director of Birmingham City FC, The Times

When I saw a full-page newspaper advertisement asking for people with experience to pass on their knowhow to the younger generation, I went to the website www.experiencecorps.co.uk and was greeted with: "The Experience Corps is an independent, non-profitmaking company, funded by a grant from the Home Office, set up to encourage people aged between 50 and 65 . . ."
Barry Holmes, retired engineer, 67, Peterborough

Eric Sykes is about to be 79. He is frail, yes. And deaf. And registered blind. And has had a quadruple heart bypass operation. But he's still impressively majestic. He has the stretching, slowly inquiring, slightly doomy head of one of those lovely, ancient sea turtles you see on wildlife programmes.
Deborah Ross, The Independent

Research carried out at the Sleep Research Centre at the University of Loughborough has revealed that lack of sleep leaves doctors and other decision-makers less able to alter

their thought processes in the light of new information. And the brain pattern of someone in their twenties who has not slept for 36 hours will have much in common with that of a 60-year-old.
The Sunday Times Style magazine

Giorgio Armani is in terrific shape. It's hard to believe that the legendary designer is now 67. Maybe he's on vitamin shots. Even his wrinkles look good. Armani genuinely seems to have attained the serenity of old age.
Melanie Rickey, Evening Standard

26 FEBRUARY 2002

Over-60s are rebelling against the label "old-age pensioner", claiming that it is patronising. They feel OAP carries with it a stigma and excludes them from the rest of society. They also think that television characters such as Victor Meldrew and EastEnder Dot Cotton do more harm than good in depicting older people. They want the word "pensioner" banned and a new term that reflects their age group better to be introduced.
Norwich Union poll

Curling has escaped the Olympic trend for ever-younger competitors: curlers are often in their late forties.
The Times

At the beginning of a holiday in St Lucia I went to the hotel spa to register for yoga classes. "Now don't worry," said the handsome young instructor with a smile as he booked me in, "we'll make them easy for you."
Maureen Pappin, 66, Hatchford, Surrey

The Australian art critic Robert Hughes, 62, has very handsome feet; no foaming yellow toenails, no crusty bunions.
Charlotte O'Sullivan, The Independent

Cindy Crawford is 36. Her light-olive skin is miraculously unlined.
Christopher Goodwin, The Sunday Times

The tide has turned in favour of experience. Doug Ellis, the Aston Villa chairman so often embroiled in tiresome battles with younger blokes who saw him as the enemy, has turned to a mate, Graham Taylor, a fellow codger . . .
Alyson Rudd, The Times, submitted by Howard Lamb, youthful codger, 58, Wargrave, Berkshire

I was offered free annual family travel insurance as a bonus for the amount that I had used on my Egg Visa card in the past year. When I read the small print I discovered that it is not available for over-65s, which Egg knows I am. After I sent several e-mails they eventually replied saying that there is no alternative offer for the over-65s. They appear to be happy taking my money, but discriminate over the bonus purely on grounds of age.
Anthony Price, Keyworth, Nottingham

5 MARCH 2002

Detailed evidence that age discrimination occurs at the heart of public policy will be published by Help the Aged tomorrow. The ground-breaking report reveals that half the population believes older people are treated as if they are on the scrapheap and a burden on society. In key areas such as health, employment, education and transport, they are second-class citizens.

The Queen gets what the Queen wants. And when she throws a pop concert at Buckingham Palace to celebrate her Golden Jubilee, she chooses who she wants to play. That might explain why Her Majesty, at 75, has hired a line-up of rock dinosaurs – with an average age of 57.
Richard Simpson, the Evening Standard

Marianne Faithfull is shorter than you thought. And more nervous than you would have imagined, at least initially. And more mumsy . . . albeit in a glamorous, fantasy-older-woman kind of way.
Garry Mulholland, Time Out

Let us hope that the sheer ludicrousness of building a drama series (*Manchild*) around the fantasies and erotic adventures of a group of middle-aged smoothies will act as aversion therapy. And that sheer public distaste will make Gene Simmons (the 52-year-old lead singer of heavy metal band Kiss who recently boasted he'd had carnal relations with more than 4,700 women) and other ageing Romeos, think twice before going intimate on us.
Terence Blacker, The Independent

HE'S HAD 4,700 WOMEN, BUT NONE OF THEM TWICE

As a local councillor I recently attended a planning meeting. Our planning officer, explaining why a housing association had placed very few car parking spaces in its plans, said: "This is because the accommodation is intended for elderly people over the age of 55."
Ian Galletley (aged 57), Darlington

Visiting a stately home near Oxford, I inquired at the gate whether there was a special entrance fee for pensioners. "Oh yes," replied the young man. "We charge them double. They take twice as long to walk round and they wear the carpets out with their shuffling feet." The mischievous gleam in his eye, plus the £2 reduction, put a smile on the face and a spring in the step of everyone in the party.
Vera Roddam Renton, Woodthorpe, Nottingham

All the signs are that Johnny Cash, 70, still has his wits about him.
Neil McCormick, The Daily Telegraph

12 MARCH 2002

Judy Finnigan is just not hungry any more. She has reached the comfort zone of middle age, where ambition has given way to dreams of retirement.
Max Davidson, Daily Mail

Raves for the over-fifties in Leeds. New 24/7 clubbing breaks based at the Village Hotel and Leisure Club aimed at fiftysomethings to prove that they still have the stamina, clothes-sense and sex appeal to keep up with young people. They will be briefed in advance on what to wear, eat, drink and say, and how to dance and look cool.
English Tourism Council's March issue of AngloFile

At 58, Malcolm McDowell is Andy Warhol meets Klaus Kinski,

unrecognisably altered from the fresh faced, tousle-haired
schoolboy of *If.* . . .
Andrew Billen, Evening Standard

Hamish Fulton is an artist who documents his solitary walks.
He comes jogging through the grey throng in electric-blue
waterproof trousers, wearing a fresh, outdoor grin. There is no
sign of breathlessness despite his 55 years.
Eve Peasnall, The Times Weekend

Joanna Lumley, who you would never guess is 60, did a lot of
filming with no make-up.
Jasper Rees, The Daily Telegraph

With reference to the search for an appropriate term to
describe us, on my 60th birthday my grandson (4 years old)
whispered in my ear: "Are you a superior citizen now?" "Yes," I
said, "I think I probably am."
Judy Chambers, Sevenoaks, Kent

Travel writer Bill Bryson, 49, is contemplating his place in
history. "I am often asked what I would like people to think of
me a hundred years from now," he says. "The best I have
come up with so far is: The amazing thing about Bill Bryson is
that he's still sexually active."
The Daily Telegraph

Notice in my Surrey gym: "Just because you're getting older
doesn't mean you can't get fit. And now you can – with our
gentle aerobics for older members. (Morning classes for those
aged 40 and over.)
Anne Morris, Reigate

19 MARCH 2002

The movies can be a mean business, especially when you turn

40. It's like we're in our prime, we're ready to rock – and they tell us to play the mother of a 20-year-old.
Rosanna Arquette, The Guardian

Warren Beatty, 65, shows that a man can spend most of his life playing the field yet still find love and have children as he moves into his pensionable years. He can have his crumpet and eat it too.
Christopher Goodwin, Evening Standard

It's funny: you watch *Space Cowboys* and even though Donald Sutherland's the baby of the cast, you realise he's an old man. He'll be 68 in July.
The Guardian Guide. Sent in by Mrs Mary Barber, Chelmsford

Christopher Walken's hair is absolutely riveting. It is thick and long and has been lovingly fashioned into three different styles: a bouffant at the front, a mullet at the back and a set of lovely flick-ups grazing his shoulders. "People always comment about my hair. It is unusual for a man of my age to have so much," he says proudly.
The Daily Telegraph

Simon Callow, who is performing *The Mystery of Charles Dickens* at the Albery Theatre, says: "Charles Dickens threw himself into performances and did it all on adrenalin. He couldn't speak for ten minutes afterwards. He was in a terrible physical state by the end of it. And he was only 58 when he died."
   Callow is about to turn 53 – isn't he alarmed?
Victoria Lambert, The Daily Telegraph

"When he is 60 she will be 86 and might be a little old lady in a home." This is the explanation given by the Reverend Ruth Wollaston, vicar of a United Reform Church in Manchester, on why she refused to marry a woman of 54 and a man of 27.
The Times

The word is that for top fashion advice, you should ask a gay man. Only If you want to make your mum happy.
Shane Watson, The Guardian

26 MARCH 2002

Sir Trevor McDonald, 62, of *News at Ten*, has been named the nation's favourite news presenter in a survey that appeared to put age and experience over youth and good looks. The BBC presenters Michael Buerk, 57, and Jeremy Paxman, 51, were second and third.
The Guardian

So high are the seats in the upper balconies that doctors in rented tuxedos will be on hand in case any of the octogenarian Academy members have difficulty in breathing after their climb.
William Cash, the Evening Standard

From an item on BBC East Midlands News: A woman aged 70 was fulfilling a lifetime ambition by learning to fence. The presenter remarked: "The nearest most 70-year-olds get to fencing is leaning on it talking to the neighbours."
Sheila Mills, Loughborough

I am a new reader of your paper and the Not Dead Yet column fills me with dismay. Here are people of 50, 60 and 70 boasting of their busy lives and presumably basking in an aura of self-satisfaction. Hence my letter headed "Disgusted". I would suggest to them that the best is still to come. I am 95.
Alec Holden, Epsom, Surrey

Norma Morgan, a retired primary school teacher from Selly Oak, Birmingham, has won a BBC radio contract after recording a monologue about how women in their sixties were

never offered sprays of the latest perfume at department store cosmetics counters. "You reach the end of what you call your working life and then you get this chance," she said.
The Daily Telegraph

Sexual deviants, cold-blood killers, steely femme fatales – Isabelle Huppert thas spent three decades carving a niche as French cinema's most beloved psychopath. And at an age when many actresses are sidelined into sexless matriarchs – she turns 47 this month . . .
Stephen Dalton, The Times (sent in by Mrs Christine Peaks, Erith, Kent)

A sandwich board outside Luton Town Hall: "Age Concern: 50-Plus drop-in centre".
Yours in angst, Denis O'Donoghue (51 and five-sixths)

2 APRIL 2002

Around three o'clock in the morning, at the underground hard-house and techno club Crash, in deepest Vauxhall, nearly 1,200 male clubbers are stripped to the waist and getting intense. On top of the beats they're dancing to the ululating wail of a 69-year-old Japanese woman . . ."
Michael Bracewell, The Independent

From the Motoring Section of *The Independent* Magazine: description by a reader of the Peugeot 607 Diesel – "I think it will appeal to people in their sixties who are retiring but still want something big. The dash is really archaic and clumsy."
From Mrs Jennifer Barnes, Surrey

Extract from *Ski Express* (a US ski magazine): "Everyone feels comfortable on the Breckenbridge ski slopes . . . but sometimes the youthful exuberance sort of clouds the brain and all of a sudden a 37-year-old guy with thinning hair, a

mortgage and two bad knees is heading full bore to the 'halfpipe' ski run. Of course there are only two possible outcomes. He'll either catch some nice air and surprise everyone or, halfway up the wall, catch a ski edge and fall. So, please, old guys, be careful out there. There's a lot to do in this town and we wouldn't want you to leave early."
From Phil Allen, Horsham, West Sussex (still skiing at 67)

An enormous number of people who think it's never going to happen are very encouraged by the fact that here is a guy to whom it happened – at 52, an age when most people have given up.
Julian Fellowes, screenwriter, Gosford Park, The Times

Am I the oldest swinger in town?
Hugh Grant, still single at 41, Evening Standard

9 APRIL 2002

Congratulations to Liz Hurley on the birth of a baby son – but at 36, is she too old to be a mum? (Freeserve's home page, April 4.)
Sent in by Martin Packer, Birmingham

Fighting Ageism: new opportunities for people over 40. This leaflet from the Third Age Foundation came through my letterbox today. Having turned 40 fairly recently, I was surprised to see that I am now "Fighting Ageism".
Gina Bentley, Ealing, London

A couple of the more strenuous, least significant routines were mimed – disgraceful yes, but then it's hard to sing and dance at the same time, especially when you are 56.
Review of Liza Minnelli in concert, Allen Robertson, The Times

From the *Computer Bulletin*, membership magazine of the

British Computer Society: "The team are not all computer scientists. They are a mix of ages – including people over 40 . . ."
Sent in by Vaughan Bishop, Kingston upon Thames

And age is no barrier to rudeness – in fact, older players tend to be the worst culprits: they indulge in the sort of infantile bickering that you normally see only in playgrounds.
Susanna Gross on octogenarian bridge players, The Spectator

At 12,000ft, the Wetterhorn is one of the biggest peaks in the Swiss Alps and a difficult climb. On June 20, 1896 Christian Almer, a leading professional guide, and his wife Margharetta celebrated their golden wedding by climbing the mountain together. Following the local practice Christian carried a young fir tree on his back. They wore their normal street clothes and the only concession to the difficulties was to wear stout boots. On that day Christian was 74, his wife 71.
Nigel Ellis, Sutton, Surrey

It was like visiting a once brilliant old aunt who had gone gaga.
George Melly on Paris, New Statesman

"She can be old, though not much older than, say, 35" – a
computer programmer talking about his ideal prostitute.
The Guardian

16 APRIL 2002

Amanda Redman, 42, star of *At Home With the Braithwaites*,
says of her relationship with marketing executive Damian
Schnabel, 29: "Damian's far more grown up than I am, so age
doesn't come into it. I think younger men find older women
interesting. They fancy them more."
Daily Mail

Ozzy Osbourne, the Birmingham-born 53-year-old former
Black Sabbath front man, has been to hell and back so often
that he has a season ticket.
Pete Clark, Evening Standard

Turning for Home by Sarah Challis is an ideal beach read, and
my mum loved it.
Jonathan Spencer-Payne, The Bookseller

Humphrey Lyttelton has not lost the will to live. He is 80,
although in his own mind his age veers. "I'm 40 onstage and
120 in Waitrose," he says.
The Daily Telegraph

Fitness for the over-50s: gym equipment for the elderly has
opened at Rushcliffe Arena.
*From the Nottingham Evening Post. Sent in by Tony Coleman,
Nottingham*

Joan Rivers, now 68 – the same age as her "best friend" Joan Collins, whom she dishes magnificently at the end of her 45-minute show – has more bounce than a pogo stick. In fact, she looks absolutely amazing: thin, trim, beautifully coiffed. Mind you, I was sitting quite a way back.
Michael Coveney, Daily Mail

Saga has come a long way since the company started offering out-of-season holidays to the over-65s in Folkestone. Now, Saga holidaymakers are five times more likely to head for Borneo than Bournemouth. Bungee jumping may not figure yet, but Saga's latest holidays are for crumbly would-be cowboys. A new 11-night holiday, Trailblazin' in the Old West, gives over-50s . . ."
Marjorie Yue in the Evening Standard. Sent in by Christine Marchant, London SE1

23 APRIL 2002

I think women are more interesting in their forties. They have lived longer; they are more confident about their choices, and they don't have to be hip and cool anymore, which I think is a godsend – you make really bad choices when you are trying to be hip.
Jodie Foster, Evening Standard

An employee arrived for work on Monday with her lower arm in a support. I asked what had happened and she said she had been experiencing some pain between her elbow and wrist. The doctor couldn't tell her what was wrong but said: "You are not 18 any more." She is 27.
Hilary Jones, London W4.

In the end, whether men of a certain age run off with one woman half our age or 20 women twice our age, whether we leave home to spend our Saturday nights emptying our wallets into the thongs of exotic dancers in a strip palace in Wichita County, or our Sunday mornings weeping through coffee concerts at the Wigmore Hall, it all comes down to the melancholy of being a man, and the further melancholy of being a man in what we now have to call late middle-age because we cannot bear to use the word "old".
Howard Jacobson, Evening Standard

Paul McCartney, in an interview on a Chicago radio station during his current tour of America: "I hope to be still singing and playing when I'm 90."
The Sun

William Boyd, the author, is an eloquently bumbling figure with the kind of proudly swept-back, receding mane that a man gets when he enters his fifties and is at peace with himself.
Tom Cox, The Daily Telegraph

". . . although she celebrates her 60th birthday this summer she is still up there partying with the best of them."
Vinny Lee on Betsey Johnson, fashion designer, The Times Magazine. Sent in by Raymond McCann, London SW2.

"Beauty fades. I just turned 29; I probably don't have that many good years left in me."
Gwyneth Paltrow, Theatregoer Magazine. Sent in by Laura McGarty, aged 14, East Grinstead

It is amusing for Celia Brayfield (T2, March 26) to blame the "popcorns" for ruining so many nights at the movies – but not accurate, in my experience. Two women of a certain age talked through *A Beautiful Mind* with the regularity of a dripping tap – whereas two teenagers who had clearly decided the film was not what they had hoped for, slipped quietly away. Several times I was brought close to tears during *Iris* – not just by the unbearable pathos, but also the crinkle of sweet wrappers. Heaven help us if they allow the oldies to slurp their tea and suck at their biscuits in the back row.
Kevin Burden, aged 39, Bristol.

30 APRIL 2002

"Once I have played Cleopatra, I know that at 54 there are no other great roles left for me to play."
Sinead Cusack in The Guardian

The National Theatre is rebranding itself for a younger audience with a five-month season called Transformations. The National's mailing-list regulars may wish to check their pacemakers before they set foot in the building this summer.
Jasper Rees, The Daily Telegraph

Perhaps James Brown, the clever Yorkshireman who gave the world *Loaded* magazine, is experiencing the sort of stuff that

usually happens when you're pushing 37? The coke takes longer to assimilate – and disperse. There are the occasional, embarrassing occurrences of penile lassitude. The belly begins to sag. There is the start of a horrible turkey-wattle around the throat.
Rod Liddle, The Guardian

The day before my 89th birthday the Fine Arts Society opened my exhibition of shellwork. A journalist rang up a friend who had been to some of my other exhibitions as she wanted to write an article. She asked how old I was and when he replied in my 90th year, she asked in amazement, "Is he still all there?"
Peter Coke, Melton Constable, Norfolk

"It is a very good year for Britain," says Simon Perry, Cannes official scout for UK films. "It proves that we are a country with some world-class film-makers. But Michael Winterbottom is a Nineties film-maker and Ken Loach and Mike Leigh are Sixties and Seventies film-makers. We must ask ourselves where the next generation is. We haven't yet got an astonishing new voice."
Evening Standard

The famous women of the Sixties seem to retain an air of youthfulness. How do you keep yours? Keep smiling – it takes ten years off.
Jane Birkin, The Independent

7 MAY 2002

While some of her fans will welcome another chance to see Cilla Black's shapely pins, others will be wondering whether a woman on the verge of her bus pass should be showing a little more decorum.
Daily Mail

When I turned 70, I thought it was time to behave with a certain gravitas. But that remains hard. I would rather be 20. Who wouldn't?
Fay Weldon in the Evening Standard

And some greybeards, fumbling with buttons, might well think there are better uses of human ingenuity than trying to click a handset and navigate past a three-headed dog called Fluffy.
Geoff Brown on the Harry Potter DVD in T2, sent in by David Trickett, London

After nine years in showbiz – I'm now 36 – I was at the height of my career, but it was soul-destroying. I couldn't do it any more. I decided to follow my heart and am now a qualified homoeopath. I am less concerned with getting old – why can't women age with dignity?
Kristiane Backer, former MTV presenter

Asda plans to recruit another 10,000 people to bring the number aged 50-plus up to 20 per cent of its staff by launching what it believes is a unique campaign. Recruitment squads will visit bingo halls, community centres, church halls and – in the words of Asda – anywhere that over-50s may frequent.
The Sunday Telegraph, sent in by David Blackburn, Derbyshire

Kiss FM's Bam-Bam is intense, neurotic, insecure, occasionally crass, but clearly a brilliant broadcaster who feels more alive on-air than in supposed real life. What will he call himself if still working at Terry Wogan's age? Zim Zim?
Evening Standard

14 MAY 2002

The Radio Joint Audience Research figures revealed that Radio 2 is the nation's most popular station and that 63-year-

old Terry Wogan's breakfast show reached a record 7.46
million listeners. He says: "It's great that Radio 2 is still rock
and rolling and proves that Coffin-dodgers still rule."
The Times

Older teachers in Scotland are to be given the chance to work
part-time from the age of 56 without any loss of pension. The
perk does not apply to teachers in England and Wales.
The Times Educational Supplement

When he went on an outing with his girlfriend Calista Flockhart
and her 16-month-old adopted son Liam, Harrison Ford proved
that even at 59 he hasn't lost the knack of keeping a toddler
entertained.
Daily Mail

As a response to the huge amount (sic) of readers who request
more styles for the older woman, we chose three ladies over
40 who all demonstrate that true style is timeless.
*From the June edition of Hair Now, sent in by Denise Taylor,
Tewkesbury*

You never normally get the chance to see an ugly woman on
TV. And the only old women you see are those who still look
lovely, such as Anna Ford and Joan Bakewell.
Mary Ann Sieghart, The Times

Visually, Vivienne Westwood's quite a turn, even at 61.
Andrew Billen, The Times

Paul Newman was 75 at the time, an age when a lot of people
can't even carry their pension books ...
*Barry Norman in the Radio Times submitted by Gill Wyatt, Margate,
Kent*

It is unquestionably true that youth is wasted on the young.
But, I am happy to report, middle age is definitely not wasted

by most people. It is cherished. And why not? It is, after all, the golden age.
Tim Lott, Evening Standard

21 MAY 2002

Sharon Stone, 44, said she planned to return to work but would now take more dignified roles than the steamier ones she is famed for. Roles that suited her age.
The Daily Telegraph

Taking up flying in your seventies, the mind boggles . . ."
Libby Purves, Midweek, Radio 4. Sent in by Dennis Smith, Chessington, Surrey

Normally the West End theatre audience is a cross between an old folk's home and a suburban bridge party. You feel that anything more taxing than Alan Ayckbourn's drawn-out TV sketches would leave them gasping for oxygen.
Michael Winner, Evening Standard

I could never be anorexic, because I would never not want to eat. But lipo would not be out of the question. Remember, I am in an industry where they eat their elders.
Dale Winton, Daily Mail Weekend

Unashamedly middle-class and sometimes over-reliant on elderly star names, Chichester Theatre has been described as "the safest house in Britain", a theatre in a green field where the sun shines on a sea of blue rinses and glints off the Zimmer frames of its ageing clientele.
Charles Spencer, The Telegraph

In a sense, Justin de Villeneuve, creator of Twiggy, is a fossilised folk hero of that heady decade the Sixties.
Dominic Lutyens, The Independent

I am not all that enamoured of Hollywood. I think that the work here is more interesting. And I am lucky to be part of the generation of actresses who have remained employed through their middle years. In the old days, you went from ingenue to old bag with a long stretch of unemployment in between.
Julie Walters, Evening Standard

Certainly Cilla Black's frenetic energy, matched by a svelte physique beneath a daring outfit of leather trousers and stilettos, are not the attributes you would normally expect to find in someone fast approaching 60.
Paul Bracchi, Daily Mail

28 MAY 2002

This is the Cliff Richard of wine, it is pretty, appealing, light and well mannered. It is not hugely fashionable – it's the sort of wine that middle-aged women will feel comfortable with.
Andrew Jefford, Evening Standard wine correspondent

Alan Walker, director of the Economic and Social Research Council's Growing Older Programme at the University of Sheffield: "As people become older, they adjust to their lower capacity and restrictions on their activities. On the whole, they are not miserable people."
The Times

At 67 years of age, Sir Roy Strong still cuts a fabulous dash . . .
Jan Moir, The Daily Telegraph

I would like to learn to ride a bike but I am 45 so I don't know how much longer I will actually be able to do these things without my bones buckling as they get old and brittle.
Frank Skinner, Metro, sent in by Sue Ash, Dudley, West Midlands

Our mother will be 100 in August. At 95 she travelled to East Germany to attend two performances of Mahler's Third Symphony (a composer she "discovered" at the age of 80). And shortly before her 97th birthday she "discovered" the late Beethoven Quartets and played them almost continually till she had thoroughly absorbed them. Is it ageist to be proud of her?
John Carew, London WC1

Sharon Stone is 44 and Madonna is 43. Both are determinedly provocative and outspoken. However, there is one big difference between them – their attitude to being middle-aged.
Shane Watson, Evening Standard

The patronising headline above Garnier's double-page advert for a "synergie lift" face cream which claims to restore firmness and elasticity proclaims: "Wrinkles don't look charming on everyone."
Most glossy magazines

4 JUNE 2002

Tony Bennett, 75: "I feel wonderful. I remember how I felt when I was 14 and I feel like that now."
The Guardian

During the Jeremy Paxman interviews, Tony Blair was emphatic about education being a priority for the Government. However, in a leaflet produced by the Department for Education and Skills, financial support for courses is available for students only up to the age of 54. People who take early retirement, or who are made redundant, may well want to enrol. They may also be facing financial hardship and would therefore be the very people who do need financial support. So where is the commitment to "lifelong learning"?
Dr Geoffrey Lloyd, Caerphilly

Since Lulu burst on the scene with the hit single *Shout* in the Swinging Sixties, she has been recycled more times than the ubiquitous crocheted miniskirt.
Paul Bracchi, Daily Mail

Considering that Ricci Burns started out in 1960 – when Victoria Beckham's mother wasn't even ten – what's left of him is in rather better shape than he has any right to expect.
Nick Foulkes, Evening Standard

Make driving tests more difficult – and include psychological testing. Increase the age for qualifying and encourage drivers of "a certain age" to forsake their licence.
Letter in The Guardian

I guess it must be very hard on him and that is why he is taking a break. I keep my fingers crossed for him. He is 45. He has not many years left – José-María Olazabal, the Spanish golfer, talking about Severiano Ballesteros.
Submitted by Nigel Springthorpe, Bletchingly, Surrey

On the front in Malta, packs of pensioners waddle like penguins past souvenir shops selling cardigans and tea towels boasting ten rules for a happy marriage, while in the sunlight, miles of varicose veins compete with the oleanders for colour against acres of concrete.
Robert Johnston, Evening Standard

11 JUNE 2002

Elaine Stritch, 77, won the best theatrical event for her one-woman confessional show *At Liberty* at the Broadway Tony awards. But her acceptance speech was cut short by CBS, who moved the cameras and drowned her words with music. "I'm very, very, very, very upset," she says. "It's pretty emotional for a woman my age to win her first Tony."
The Guardian

The statistics for prostate cancer are chastening for any man, but the news is not all bad. The vast majority of cases affect the elderly (95 per cent of cases occur in men over the age of 60).
Charlotte Cripps, The Independent. Sent in by Paul Kinnear, London SW7

IT'S THE WATERWORKS

Conservative MPs in their 60s are under orders to declare swiftly if they will not stand again to allow associations to select younger candidates to lead grassroots campaigning. Iain Duncan Smith wants a new generation of Conservative MPs more in tune with the population at large.
The Times

Seen on a poster at the B&Q store, junction 9, M6, Walsall: Coming soon, Golden Oldies Club, for ladies and gentlemen over 50.
Pat Anderson, Walsall, West Midlands

Simon Reed, commentating on the French Open Tennis Tournament on the satellite channel British Eurosport, said, after a particularly good rally in a men's match between Grosjean (France) and Clavet (Spain) in which the point was won by the Spaniard: "He shouldn't be able to run about like that; after all, he is 33."
Michael Pollock, Selsdon, Surrey

Athletic feat of the day: Cesare Maldini. On the day that he became the oldest person to lead a team in the World Cup finals, the Paraguay coach belied his 70 years, leaping about wildly as his team took a two-goal lead against South Africa.
The Times, World Cup section, June 3. Sent in by Dennis Smith, Chessington, Surrey

18 JUNE 2002

Emily Bearn, the 27-year-old who lives with Lucian Freud, 79, is no stranger to relationships that are not so much May-September as January-December . . . Like Heather Mills with Sir Paul McCartney, Bearn's predilections give hope to bus-pass lotharios everywhere.
Dan Cairns, Evening Standard

... FORGIVE US OUR BUS PASSES ...

The closure of retirement homes puts an awful lot of large houses, some quite grand, back on the market, and if you can banish the ubiquitous linoleum handrails and whiff of lavender water (or something worse?) you might have yourself a bargain."
The Sunday Times homes supplement. Sent in by June Benn, London

The Miss Marple lookalike was a neighbour from hell. Instead of growing old gracefully she grew cannabis . . . Whatever happened to the little old ladies who needed a hand to cross the road?"
Emma Jones, The Sun

Most 59-year-olds are ready for their carpet slippers and pipe.
Nina Myskow, aged 56, speaking on The Jimmy Young Show, Radio 2. Sent in by Angela Cotton, Bournemouth, Dorset

25 JUNE 2002

Being a French drama, sex is never far away and, even as she heads for 60, Catherine Deneuve makes a creditable onscreen love object.
Sean Macaulay, The Times

A 71-year-old cancer patient, raped in a mixed sex ward, was called "a silly old woman" and ordered back to bed after she told a nurse of the assault.
Daily Mail

Performing at the Sheffield Arena, Rod Stewart looked like an over-excited roué in the final minutes before being ejected from Tramp.
Tom Horan, The Daily Telegraph

Pensioners are by far the worst drivers. They are spiteful, dithering, old and in the way. They should have their licences taken away.
Jeremy Clarkson, who had just pranged a £50,000 Ford RS200, reported in the Daily Mail. Sent in by Margaret Dunbar, Edinburgh

At 83, Donald T. Regan, Ronald Reagan's former chief of staff, has become a celebrated landscape artist. "Nine years ago I

thought 'retirement is starting to irritate me. There is more to life than golf, the stock market and drinking'."
Financial Times

Since the Moon, I have been searching for my next mountain. I have found a few hills, but nothing else. However, I am now the grandfather of nine grandchildren, so that is something.
Eugene Cernan, 68, the last man to walk on the Moon, The Observer Magazine

I recently inquired about a mortgage at one of the high-street lenders. The mortgage adviser greeted me with: "Obviously, not a first-time buyer." She then solicitously asked me whether I thought I would be able to cope with the short flight of steps up to her office. I am 49.
Stephen Shaw, London

2 JULY 2002

The Times columnist Simon Barnes on England's quarter-final debacle: "Seaman was simply gobsmacked by the shot . . . his mind did not react. The minds of 38-year-olds are not as supple as they once were."
Jackie Banerjee, Walton-on-Thames

There is an over-50s dating site which provides single men and women with their own, exclusive online dating agency. In addition to editorial, the site also offers a range of products that are tailored to the needs of over-50s, like gardening products, health supplements, and so on.
Manchester Evening News. Sent in by Graham Nicholson, Alderley Edge, Cheshire

Joan Rivers says that she still feels about 30, and all her friends tend to be younger than her. Getting old is horrible.

"The worst thing is that you are invisible. You don't get the jobs you should be getting and you go to a party and you are a non-person, especially to the opposite sex."
Evening Standard

Nicky Haslam may be in his 60s but . . .
Daily Mail

"I suppose that at 56 I should have known better" – Mrs Eileen Watkis on being taken in by pyramid selling.
Evening Standard

"Vanessa Redgrave is unstooped and remains fine-featured, but at 64, in her sensible specs, she will soon be able to pass herself off as an old lady."
Andrew Billen, The Times

According to Blockbuster, *Dr Zhivago* (1965) is still considered the most romantic movie.
News of the World

"There will be a sequel to this book if I live long enough" – final words in Cecilia Jenkin's first book, *Memories of a Welsh Woman*, published by Green Dragon Press and set up by Mrs Jenkin on her own computer (Mrs Jenkin is 96).
Wyn Jones, Narberth, Pembrokeshire

9 JULY 2002

I was 56 when I hit America (well beyond graveyard time for female hosts). I worry constantly about my fat thighs and my "Camilla crevices" on each side of my mouth.
Anne Robinson, in The Independent Review

The UN recently hosted an international conference on one of the greatest current threats to society. The subject had nothing

to do with international terrorism, nor did global warming get a mention. The very real menace facing our planet is old age.
Paul Groves, in The Birmingham Post. Sent in by Dr Peter Taylor, Edgbaston, Birmingham

The Stones seem, for several decades now, to have been trying to ignore the fact that they are old men. The sight of the wrinkled fop Jagger flouncing round the stage, wiggling his bottom and clapping his hands like a fey flamenco dancer, has become one of rock's greatest embarrassments.
Andy Gill, in The Independent Review

The key to popularity changes with each generation: if you're a teenager, be cool and hang out; if you're in your twenties, be fun and party; if you're any older, just be nice and put the kettle on.
Guy Browning, in Guardian Weekend. Sent in by Judy Chambers, Sevenoaks, Kent

England struck forward with about as much drive and inspiration as a middle-aged couple in a Morris Minor. The Koreans have been beaten twice in everything but name. That, after being given more outside assistance towards an earlier victory than an old man in a wheelchair would need to climb Mount Everest.
Jeff Powell, in the Daily Mail. Sent in by Arthur Green, Hemel Hempstead

You face certain things as you get older and think "Well, time is running out". I do like to keep the brain working. I learn poetry for that. And playing the piano is a good mental and physical exercise in co-ordination.
Anthony Hopkins, in the Evening Standard

Katie Jarvis, in *Cotswold Life*, June: "When we arrive an older couple are at the only other occupied table, chatting animatedly. They can't be married – at least not to each other –

I decide. In my experience, conjoined couples of that age generally sit in silence, albeit a comfortable, warm-slipper type of silence."
Kenneth Rathborne, Chipping Campden

16 JULY 2002

Dolly Parton is 56 years old, but she doesn't look it. It is not that she looks younger; she just somehow doesn't seem to manifest any of the normal outward indicators used to assess age.
Oliver Burkeman, The Guardian

In the past year or so I have received frequent exhortations to pay for my funeral in advance and to make legacies to charities. I am 93 and wonder if there is some trigger date registered somewhere for the starting up of these mailings?
Lesley Lewis, London SW3

Vanessa Redgrave looks her 65 years, yet her beauty is somehow undiminished.
Brian Viner, The Independent

Possibly young men are the only ones able to accept power and authority in women as an aphrodisiac rather than a threat. If so, there may be a whole new future for those great actresses in their late thirties and forties and fifties to whom Hollywood said a cruel and premature goodbye.
Molly Haskell, The Guardian

Bryan Ferry's vanity is celebrated and still going strong, despite his being 56.
Simon Mills, The Sunday Times Style magazine

Macleans has specially developed a new toothpaste to fight the problems of maturing teeth and gums. It is called 40+.
Waitrose Selections magazine

The latest statistics from the British Household Panel Survey and the US Census confirm that another sexual revolution is under way: middle-class women, vastly more economically and sexually independent than their mothers, are turning to toy boys.
The Sunday Times

TOYBOYS 'Я' US

23 JULY 2002

Two doughty British Airways stewardesses aged 55 and 54 are demanding to carry on working until they are 60. Without beating about the bush, do we want women of advanced years showing us to our seats on aeroplanes? Do we want our lifejackets demonstrated by women old enough to be our mothers? Do we want to be offered canapés by grey-haired battleaxes who have been in the job so long they can hardly conceal their boredom?
Max Davidson, the Daily Mail

I contemplated buying a new cream that claimed to stop the seven signs of ageing and wondered what they might be. Incontinence? Talking about the weather? Wearing slippers? Memory loss? Compulsive need to queue up at the post office? Memory loss? Inability to comprehend the lyrics of pop songs?
Maria McErlane, The Sunday Times

WHY DON'T YOU
WEAR SENSIBLE
SHOES?

Richard Widmark, aged 87: "I don't know how many years I have left, so I thought we might as well make the trip to London in real comfort on the QE2."
The Daily Telegraph

I have decided to lie about my age because I am fed up with having to listen to people's silences when they learn my true age. What's a date got to do with whether or not I work out in the gym, have an opinion about Eminem or try to pull a man they all fancy?
Mary Russell, The Guardian

Flavio Briatore has never done a drug in his life, but when I made a decision that I didn't want to live that life any more, he was the first person I told. He found a place for me to go and

came with me. And you know, he's 51 years old, and for him to try to understand all this is tough.
Naomi Campbell, The Daily Telegraph

I am 56 years old, an age when many women tend not to be noticed as we plod about in our comfortable extra wide, midi-heeled sensible shoes. Many of my contemporaries have terrible feet, deformed by bunions, permanent corns and layers of dead skin like rock strata.
Sue Townsend, The Independent

Recently, at the age of 71, I applied for a one-year writing fellowship at Cambridge. When, owing to an obvious oversight, I was not shortlisted, I was consoled by a friend. "Never mind," he said, "maybe they wanted someone a bit older."
Fred Holland, Coventry

30 JULY 2002

Saggy arms and wrinkled legs wouldn't normally merit a second glance in a 69-year-old woman. But when the woman is Joan Collins, eyebrows are inevitably raised, for the actress had seemingly retained her stunning looks and flawless skin well into pensionable age. But in a daring white swimming costume there was proof she has not escaped the ravages of old age. She has clearly suffered the same kind of ageing as ordinary mortals.
Daily Mail

From "Two Brains" by Raymond Keene in *The Times*: "An ancient Greek lived one-fourth of his life as a boy, one-fifth as a youth, one-third as a man and spent the last 13 years of his life as an elderly gent. How old was he when he died?" The answer is 60 (he was an "elderly gent" at 47).
Sent in by several readers

The seaside village of Mumbles is a pretty, prosperous and a mildly pretentious place. It's an odd place to have produced a theologian of any kind, let alone one of Rowan Williams's provoking power. There is a hedonism in the air on summer nights, when the retired are abed.
Hywel Williams, The Guardian

"Pretty wrinkly woman" – headline over a picture of 34-year-old Julia Roberts which shows she has a few laughter lines around her eyes.
News of the World

As a child I always found it difficult to eat cereal without spilling milk down my chin or splashing it on my shirt. Now, at the age of 70, I am still prone to the same mistakes. At breakfast my six-year-old granddaughter, said: "You are slurping." I explained that I had had this problem since I was a child. She thought about this, then said: "That isn't why. You slurp because you are old."
Sir John Mayhew-Sanders, Umberleigh, Devon

In they hobbled to the Sex Pistols' Golden Jubilee concert, the original fans, old now but basking in memories of 1977, punk rock's long, hot summer of hate.
Evening Standard

Harrison Ford, with his ear stud and inappropriately younger partner, Calista Flockhart, needs someone to slap him round the face with an order of sushi before he falls too deeply into the theatre of the male menopause.
Tim Lott, Evening Standard

"Inevitably I'm being given a hard time for being a typical ageing male, going off and packing in the wife."
Rick Stein, The Mail on Sunday

6 AUGUST 2002

I look at the women in Hollywood, my age or a little older, who do not accept their age, physically. They start doing things to their face and body which are designed to make them look less than their real age. They feel pressure to play women who are younger. I don't think it is worth trying to look ten years younger through surgery. It is too high a price to pay.
Debra Winger, 47, Saga magazine

After I designed one of the Indiana Jones films for Steven Spielberg, I was taken aback, when reading the publicity material, to see that the section devoted to me started "Veteran designer Anthony Powell . . .At the time I was 45.
Anthony Powell, Blackheath, London

Roberto Cavalli seems embarrassed at the comparison with Gianni Versace, but realises, even at his age (62), his own potential to fill the great man's shoes.
Heath Brown, Times Magazine

In front of the floating stage, women and men, many over the age of 40, when common sense should have told them not to, danced and bopped throughout the whole performance (at the Henley Festival).
The Henley Standard, sent in by Val Murphy

Kate Matthews, 68, from Dover, told how she was recruited in a pub by a bootlegger to help him to smuggle cigarettes across the Channel. "Which Customs man is going to stop a car with a white-haired old lady eating a box of Belgian chocolates and waving to them?" she said.
The Times

According to Anna Wintour, the Editor of American *Vogue*, her creative director, Grace Coddington, "has a body of work

unmatched by any other fashion editor because she has the best eye in the business. She can sense a trend before the designers have an inkling of what's going on." With that kind of praise, it's no wonder that, even aged 60, Coddington is still the high priestess of fashion.
Colin McDowell, The Sunday Times

Paul Sidney has shaped the WLNG radio station into a profitable and award-winning enterprise with a series of offbeat decisions. In the early Sixties, Sidney dubbed WLNG "The Oldies Station", despite a consultant's warning that the phrase connoted obsolescence and death.
The New Yorker, sent in by Mike Popham, Surrey

The claims that baby-boomers make for themselves – that they invented teenagehood, the Pill, rock'n'roll, indeed anything pertaining to enjoyment of a generally sexual nature – make them difficult to like en masse.
Zoe Williams, The Guardian

13 AUGUST 2002

Should women bare all? In response to pictures of Ulrika Jonsson appearing topless last week Winifred Robinson proclaimed: "It is evident that Ulrika Jonsson has not been surgically enhanced, but in her late thirties, and after two children, she has a figure that many teenage girls would envy, let alone women approaching middle age."
Daily Mail

I have recently noticed that you are no longer wanted if you are over 80. Insurance adverts, medical surveys, etc, all end at 80. Even in our local surgery the cricket club is advertising for new members: "We could have a team that will suit you – 8 to 80." What is wrong with us?
Ruth Sofie Sellers, Ingatestone, Essex

How to look Halli-well. Take tips from Geri on how to stay young after you've hit 30.
Headline on advice page in News of the World magazine

Carol Midgley, *The Times*, reviewing *Under the Knife* on ITV1:
Bruce, 57, was a perma-tanned divorcé who drove a red sports car and once made a Sixties pop record. He wanted surgery to remove the "shopping bags" under his eyes. "If you are going to be in a disco you don't want to feel people are looking at you thinking, 'what's that old geezer doing leaping around trying to pretend he's 20 years old?'" Bruce, Bruce. Apart from the fact that you should be buying an orthopaedic mattress rather than a facelift at your age . . .
Sent in by Cliff Michelmore, 82, Petersfield, Hampshire

Our plastic surgeon Alex Karidis says: Paul McCartney desperately needs a facelift and to have his eyes done. He is getting craggy and his jawline and neck are going. His eyes are droopy and he has developed saggy, hamster-like pouches round his mouth.
Daily Mail

Adam Faith is only 42, it's Terry Nelhams-Wright who is 62. I compartmentalise these things because you want to keep your sanity, don't you?
Adam Faith, born TN-W, in the Evening Standard

20 AUGUST 2002

In the August issue of *Elle* magazine in an interview with Calista Flockhart: "So, Ally is over, I say, studying those soulful, saucer eyes and that oh-so familiar heart-shaped face (which, for the record, is fantastically unlined for a 37 year-old)."
Fantastically?
Deborah Marson, St Albans

In these PC times you don't make racist jokes, or sexist jokes, or jokes about disabilities, but you can be as ageist as you like.
Nicholas Parsons, 73, The Daily Telegraph

If you are so worried that you have to cut your face up to make yourself happier, you're with the wrong guy.
Jerry Hall, The Sunday Times

It cannot be good for the future of English cricket when counties snap up ageing Test players. The ageing player referred to in *The Times* is Mushtaq Ahmed who is 32.
Anthony Roberts, Shoreham, Sussex

The rock wrinklies: Sting is looking better with every step he takes, even at 50; Tom Jones has become a Sex Bomb at the venerable age of 62; Elton John is still standing after all these years; Eurythmic Dave Stewart might wish he was 25, not a grand old 50.
Daily Mail

Heidi Range, of the Sugababes: "Kylie Minogue has a really good bum. She has a nice figure, especially for her age. I mean she's like 34 and she looks amazing."
Daily Mail, sent in by Mrs Hunter-Rowe, Dorking

Picture caption in *The Daily Telegraph* magazine: Diane Keaton revels in the perks of being a fiftysomething actress – no one cares what you look like.
Clive Burton, London N10

This was the night when three thirtysomething crocks rediscovered their magic. . .
The Times Sports section. The three "crocks" referred to are: Steve Backley, Kelly Holmes and Ashia Hansen. Joy Roffey, Tunbridge Wells, Kent

27 AUGUST 2002

"People try to erase the suffering they've had, but an actor's face is more touching if there's life and experience in it. I look at my mother who is 87 and I see a powerful woman. She never had a facelift."
Sigourney Weaver, 53, The Express

Every man of any age group who has ever gone out with someone who has a stunning mother will have had fantasies about her. Older women have this inner self-confidence and are confident with their bodies. I find that sexy in a woman. She has been through different experiences and come out the other side. If your girlfriend's mum is attractive – not that you would ever do anything about it, perish the thought – you just think to yourself: "Wow, she is good looking."
Nick Bailey, 30, Sunday Mirror (Dr Anthony Trueman in EastEnders)

People I work with say, "You're an old woman. My God! Get your slippers back on." All I ever want is a game of Scrabble.
Kylie Minogue, 34, Sunday Mirror

"Hollywood blockbusters in particular are targeted towards core audiences of 16 to 25-year-olds. This group is young and therefore it is accepted in the industry that they want young, sexy actors and actresses to watch, relate to and to buy into their lifestyle. Older males are still desirable to young women but the reverse is not true."
Leon Forde, reporter and assistant features editor of Screen International in The Express

"She (Catherine Zeta-Jones) looks like Sophia Loren on steroids. She's trussed up like a 50-year-old which is a shame because she's so beautiful, petite and delicate"
Susannah Constantine, presenter of the BBC show What Not

to Wear, on the 32-year-old Welsh actress who has signed a
multi-million dollar contract to be the face of Elizabeth Arden
Daily Mirror

So much for all our assumptions about dear old grey-haired
granny, basking in the presence of her children's babies in the
twilight of her days. Granny is far more likely these days to be
expensively tinted, toned and busy and suffering from a new
social disorder – acute granny rage. Older women seem
increasingly angry that their daughters and daughters-in-law
feel they have an unquestioned claim on their time as
childminders. It infuriates them still more to be made to feel
that grannies who challenge that assumption are unnatural and
unloving or, worse still, selfish. This cunning plan seems to
arouse particular resentment and one can see why. It is an
obvious form of exploitation, made all the worse for being
taken for granted.
Minette Marrin, The Sunday Times

3 SEPTEMBER 2002

I'm going to be an old-age pensioner in January, which is quite
daunting. I would never let a plastic surgeon touch me. I have
always liked elderly people, I love what they have learnt and I
want to be able to read them in their face. Or does this sound
like I'm in total denial? I do sometimes catch sight of myself in
the mirror and think, "Oh my God . . ."
Jill Kennington, The Independent

I have built and run two companies of my own, managed other
people's, been a consultant and have an MBA. Now 54, I
approached recruitment consultants. "No chance whatsoever
at your age," I was told. The consultant then added: "Do you
know what they say to MBAs in America? 'Burger and large
fries please'." He thought it was hilarious.
David C. Jaundrell, Telford, Shropshire

"I have grown up a lot since Bond," says Izabella Scorupco, who appeared in *GoldenEye*. "I am realistic about living in Hollywood and being part of the Los Angeles movie system. If I am still working at 40, I will be lucky."
Culture, The Sunday Times

One Saturday we decided, with two friends, that we would like to go to a midnight movie at the local cinema. I rang to book the seats and mentioned that we were all OAPs. "Madam," was the reply, "there are no reductions at this time of night – you should all be in bed."
Anne Phillips, Stock, Essex

Pensioners in Britain are more physically active in their everyday lives than teenagers, according to a study carried out by Dr Kimberly Fisher, of the Institute for Social and Economic Research at the University of Essex.
The Sunday Times

I think a lot about getting old. I don't want to be one of those 70-year-olds who still wants lots of sex.
Rupert Everett, Culture, The Sunday Times

Sex appeal is 50 per cent what you've got and 50 per cent what people think you've got.
Sophia Loren, 68, at the Venice Film Festival

I listen to myself walking down a London pavement to a brisk click-clack, click-clack, and I feel filled with a certitude that there is a virtue in speed. Those sauntering tourists, those doddery pensioners . . .
Mary Ann Sieghart, The Times

10 SEPTEMBER 2002

In the mid-1980s John Paul II had already survived the

attempted assassination, but in his mid-sixties he was a
surprisingly youthful man, full of mental and physical energy.
William Rees-Mogg, The Times, sent in by Jim Whyatt (82),
Wiveliscombe, Somerset

The Court of Justice of The European Communities in
Luxembourg is organising an open competition, based on
tests, for the constitution of a reserve list for future recruitment
of conference interpreters. Requirements: a candidate must be
a national of one of the Member States of the European
Community and be less than 45 years of age.
Advertisement in The Times, sent in by Margaret F. de Wolf,
Halywell, Flintshire

Waspish style counsellor Trinny Woodall: "And a word to the
wise: women over 40 should really not be wearing leather
trousers."
From the Radio Times, sent in by Mrs M. Jones, Cardiff (70, 5ft 3in,
7st 4lb)

There is no reason why Duncan Breeze should not use this
well-put-together vehicle to one day secure a major starring
role in the West End. At 26 he still looks incredibly young . . .
Review from The Stage, sent in by Bob Somerville, Edinburgh

So, clean from booze and drugs, and devoid of sleaze
(children rather than groupies in evidence), Sir Mick and his
septuagenarian beat combo Zimmered on stage in Boston on
the first leg of the Rolling Stones' latest world tour.
Will Self, Evening Standard

"If the doctors are right and we are going to live to 125 years of
age, perhaps I had better invest in a new pair of golf shoes. I'm
only 92."
Songwriter and former actor Neal Arden, of Northwood, Middlesex, in
the press release for his latest composition

17 SEPTEMBER 2002

"You were the oldest in the group, but you have still managed to do very well." (my italics) Said to Tony Blackburn, on the occasion of his winning the jungle celebrity survivor contest, by Ant or Dec (which is which?).
Andy Rodgers, Sheffield

Among the ageing Hollywood stars desperately seeking franchiseable characters is Harrison Ford, 60 . . .
Neil Norman, Evening Standard

"It was Elvis Presley's misfortune to linger into middle age with the unbecoming afflictions of old age," (Philip Norman, comparing Presley's death at the age of 42 with Eddie Cochran, Buddy Holly and James Dean, who died "at the flashy apogee of young fame".)
The Sunday Times, sent in by Mike Cumming, Bournemouth

As I was saying, 34 is a good age to get your skates on if you want a baby. Heather Mills-McCartney's husband is 60, and 60 is, well, quite old.
India Knight, The Sunday Times

Sean Newsom on the Best Hotels Awards 2003: "If Kirrough House were judged purely by the quality of its standard rooms, it would never make the grade. When I first saw it, I hated everthing about it: the bed was soft, the decor was dull and the furniture seemed to have come straight from a pensioner's bungalow."
The Sunday Times, sent in by Harry Whitehouse, Newark

As patron of the splendidly titled Not Old, Just Older awards (nojos), I invite you to nominate a special someone (secretly). We are looking for people in sport, quality of life, outstanding

achievement, consumer services, intergeneration, schools and international achievement. Write to: Emma McSweeney, Help the Aged, 207-221 Pentonville Road, London N1 9UZ.
Cherie Booth, QC

The sight of four very old men (the Rolling Stones) in skin-tight leopard-skin jeans, holding Fender Zimmer-casters to stop themselves falling over is the most hilarious comedic vignette imaginable.
Victor Lewis-Smith, London Evening Standard

24 SEPTEMBER 2002

"I am devastated at what has happened." Diana Rigg, 64, means the fate of most women in Britain, even beautiful ones like her, when they hit middle age. "I have completely disappeared. I am totally invisible. I never really liked my sexy label but on the other hand, to disappear so totally is quite startling."
Daily Mail

Seen on a T-shirt worn by a mature gentleman on a beach in Ibiza. "The older I get, the better I was."
Avice M. Stewart, Fareham, Hants

Radio 1 has been overtaken in popularity by Radio 2, once a byword for cardigan-wearing middle age, but now listened to by 13 million people.
Jessica Hodgson, Evening Standard

Kate Beckinsale is even prettier than you expect. Her complexion is flawless, the hair and make-up magazine-cover perfect. Her smile really does lighten up her face, making her look years younger than 28.
Pippa Smith, Evening Standard

The Handyperson Scheme has been supporting the community for seven years and is able to provide a wide range of practical help in elderly people's homes, where the clients are 55-plus and no longer capable of undertaking simple tasks for themselves . . .
The Berkhamsted Review, sent in by Richard Fleet, Berkhamsted, Herts

My daughter, Rachel Lawrence, a fellow barrister, came back to chambers from court one day and told me she had just been appearing for a defendant who said: "I'm so glad I've got you defending me, Miss Lawrence, because your dad used to defend my dad."
Sir Ivan Lawrence, QC, Temple, London

MY DAD CAN DEFEND YOUR DAD !

At 76, I was told by an animal rescue organisation that I was too old to have a puppy. I could not, they said, have a dog under six years old. I went to a breeder instead and now Coco is a very young six and my wife and I are fairly young at 81 and 82 respectively.
George Belbin, Norton sub Hamdon, Somerset

1 OCTOBER 2002

When I go in taxis, the first thing they say is: "Hello Eric, I thought you were dead."
Eric Sykes in The Barker, the Variety Club's magazine

Why would I want to celebrate my 60th birthday? I can't think of any reason to call this a landmark in my life, thank you very much.
Britt Ekland, Daily Mail

"Aren't you beginning to feel your age?" I ask 59-year-old Michael Palin.
Cassandra Jardine, The Daily Telegraph

Harry Winston's baubles adorn the shrivelled necks of many old trouts at the Oscars.
Daily Mail

Shuffling imperceptibly from the status of enfant terrible towards that of grand old man, Robert Wilson, 61 . . .
Dominic Cavendish, The Daily Telegraph

I'm constantly surprised at the amazing way the brain can adapt. I believe it's one of the few parts of our bodies that really does get better with age. While everything else begins to sag and slip, the brain just becomes more individual as time goes on.
Professor Susan Greenfield, Good Housekeeping

Rod Stewart, 57, has been looking for a home in the South of France, which is eminently sensible as folks of his age should park themselves in warm climes whenever possible.
The Sunday Times Home section

8 OCTOBER 2002

"With life expectancy of 80 or more today, we will be young for less than a third of that time and for most of our lives will be classed as middle-aged. I'm not keen on that description." Middle-aged at 69? Is there going to be any time of life when Joan Collins will describe herself as old?
Melanie McDonagh, Evening Standard

Men of my age are just too old, and younger ones may have the energy but they don't have the intellect.
Cilla Black, Daily Mail

The almost-octogenarian painter Lucian Freud is well known for having an extremely young girlfriend. I watched him dash across a busy main road at Notting Hill Gate and was impressed that someone so advanced in years could perform this athletic feat. No wonder he is such an old goat.
Christopher Silvester, Spectator Diary. Sent in by Dennis Smith, Chessington, Surrey

The consultant informed me that I was an "NSC" when I was pregnant with my first baby. He explained that it meant "no spring chicken". In this age of working mothers, I didn't consider 33 to be "over the hill" for my first baby.
Mrs Caroline Vincent, Barnt Green, Worcestershire

The Stone Roses' John Squire, with his tousled hair still intact at 39 . . .
Dave Simpson, The Guardian

I'm too beat-up and old now to be a sex symbol.
Mel Gibson, Daily Mail

15 OCTOBER 2002

Kim Wilde has returned to her natural mouse brown and is now a womanly Juno rather than a girlish sylph. And she's still beautiful at 41.
From Woman and Home, sent in by Joan Eadington, Penrith, Cumbria

Beautiful shoes demand beautiful feet . . . so if summer's end sees you with the feet of a 90-year-old, get thee to Norma Newman. She has a magic potion that melts away that ugly, hard, cracked skin around your heels and toes.
Olivia Lichtenstein, The Times Magazine. Sent in by Alison Goldsmith, Wimbledon, London

Mrs Caroline Vincent, from Barnt Green, Worcestershire (Not Dead Yet, Oct 8) should count herself lucky to be referred to only as "no spring chicken" when she is 33. When I was having my first child in 1978, I was 27 and the consultant said to a group of students ". . . and this is our most elderly primigravida . . ."
Nicole Jokiel, Alton, Hampshire

Connie Cox, 80, B&Q's oldest female member of staff, helped to open the DIY chain's eighth store in China. Recruited at the age of 68, Connie was promised the trip to China three years ago on the proviso that she was still with B&Q when she turned 80.

22 OCTOBER 2002

Students at St Andrews, including Prince William, will be voting for their new rector later this month. Vying to replace him are the former Liberal MP Sir Clement Freud and Germaine Greer, 63. "Clement is an old friend and I love him dearly – and

beating up an old man would not be nice," Greer said. "But if I am beaten by a 78-year-old, I don't know what that says about me."
The Daily Telegraph

With youth and vitality associated with success, people as young as 20 are gripped by a fear of ageing, say researchers.
Daily Mail

Asda plans to take on 3,300 over-fifties this Christmas, according to the *Daily Star*. "Asda wants wrinkly staff to help out over the busy festive period," the newspaper tells its readers. Tony Blair will be 50 soon: will it describe him as our wrinkly PM?
Stephanie Jenkins, Oxford,

In Hollywood the second worst sin is to be old; the worst is to look old.
From And Why Not? by Barry Norman. Sent in by Nigel Watson, Plymouth

Harrison Ford is thinking of picking up the bullwhip again for *Indiana Jones IV*. He is 60 and should know better.
Nicholas Glass, Channel 4 News. Sent in by Carol Kellman, Bury St Edmunds, Suffolk (I'm 56 and would happily hold his bullwhip).

29 OCTOBER 2002

As you get older, you don't get as horny – I don't take as many cold showers a day as I used to.
Tom Jones in the Evening Standard

It is reported that the BBC is paying £10 million for the right to screen the *Harry Potter* movie. Who needs it on TV? House-bound oldies who can't work a video recorder?
Alan Massie, The Scotsman, sent in by Irma Ireland, Edinburgh

Some of those who know Richard Madeley and Judy Finnigan use the phrase "mid-life crisis" to explain why they made the suprising move to Channel Four. There was some hostility from some executives to having the middle-aged couple (he is 46, she 54) on a station that was supposed to be youthful and cutting-edge. Worse still, the audience for their sofa slot is overwhelmingly biased towards a rump of heavy-viewing 55-plus women – hardly the kind of viewers that the station covets.
Alison Boshoff, Daily Mail

"Modelling is different when you are an old wrinkly like me. Now it's all a bit of a Jolly," says Inès de la Fressange, 45.
The Daily Telegraph

On radio, at least we won't be able to tell if Johnny Rotten's bondage trousers of the punk era have been replaced with a comfy cardigan.
Evening Standard

5 NOVEMBER 2002

It's got to be said, it's not easy strip-searching pensioners – all those flaps of skin!
The comedian Ross Noble on Have I Got News For You, sent in by Janet Taylor, Totnes, Devon

Exhibiting extensive expertise in every rock and roll move in the book, Bruce Springsteen swung from his microphone stand, danced on the piano and slid across the stage on his knees, a daring manoeuvre for any 53-year-old.
David Smyth, Evening Standard

Barry Humphries, 68, is at his best confronting uncomfortable truths, and age has not mellowed him much.
Sarah Sands, The Daily Telegraph

The dosage instructions on a packet of Sainsbury's paracetamol tablets says: "Adults, the elderly, and children over 12 years . . .They give no clue as to when one crosses over from being adult to elderly.
Richard Iley, Birmingham

It was the last thing any woman would expect a man to do at his age.
Louisa Moore, on being dumped by the former James Bond actor, Roger Moore, 75, in the Daily Mail

Unlike Ursula Andress, the Aston Martin DB5 still looks fresh today.
Headline in The Sunday Times's James Bond supplement, sent in by Mervyn Coverdale, Maidstone, Kent

12 NOVEMBER 2002

Kenneth Clarke, 62, above, is accused of being "an old man in a hurry for the leadership".
The Times

"Television in particular seldom has any use for those who are in the autumn of their years."
Victor Lewis-Smith, Evening Standard

"I think it's very important to keep some of our nonagenarians because there is no one more immune to the power of patronage; even death does not frighten them any more. Some of the best people are over 70."
Lord Russell, 65, in the House of Lords debate

"I do watch my weight, especially if I've got to get into a bikini, and as you get older it all gets that bit wobblier."
Calvin Klein model Lisa Ratcliff, 22, in The Sunday Times. From Christine Hemsley, Nottinghamshire

To an 80-year-old urgently needing heating repairs under a maintenance contract: "You can have priority only if there is a serious water leak or you are over 90."
British Gas call centre

"When I was young, people of 51 were old. But now I am 51, it doesn't seem old."
Phil Collins, The Independent

19 NOVEMBER 2002

"You don't sound that old. You sound full of life." Jonathan Ross, on Radio 4, to a caller in her early sixties.
From Richard Ogilvy, Forres

"I came to a love of Wagner late in life. The magic of it all did not really hit me until I was 40 . . ."
A. N. Wilson, The Daily Telegraph. From David Wood

"As you grow old, you lose your interest in sex, your friends drift away, your children often ignore you. There are many other advantages, of course, but these would seem to be the outstanding ones."
Richard Needham, Toronto Globe and Mail. From Julian Corlett, Scunthorpe

"Most of the deaths are among the elderly, but that really means anybody over 50."
Professor Keatinge of Queen Mary's School of Medicine, in an article on winter health in Sainsbury's Magazine. From Barbara Jukes, Northampton

"Now, when we launch new companies, the need to make a fool of myself is slightly less. Maybe I'll be allowed to grow old with dignity."
Sir Richard Branson, 52. For the launch of Virgin Broadband internet he dressed in red lycra

"She's so beautiful. I expected her to be a bit wrinkly, because she's 30-odd, but she wasn't."
Kate Lewis of Fame Academy on Mariah Carey. From Heather Jeffery, Bristol

26 NOVEMBER 2002

Pierce Brosnan on nearing 50: "The older you get, the stronger you have to get. Getting old is not for sissies."
The Mail on Sunday, sent in by Margaret Ward, Beer, Devon

A *Daily Express* reader called Joe, on the subject of nostalgia, laments that, when he pays his barber, he is no longer asked: "Anything for the weekend, sir?"

Columnist David Robson replied: "Do you think it could be because you won't see 75 again?"

ANYTHING FOR THE YEAR END, SIR?

No decision has yet been taken on who is to be the new Miss Marple, but Prunella Scales, Maggie Smith and Julie Walters have all been suggested for the part. "Luckily in Britain there is

no dearth of old, posh actresses," John Whiston, head of drama at Granada, said.
Sent in by Jane Kime, Wisbech, Cambridgeshire

Most nursing home deaths are caused by neglect traced to care-givers whom the elderly rely on for food and liquid, and for turning them in their beds. The latest compilation of more than 500,000 nursing home deaths – for 1999 – lists starvation, dehydration or bedsores as the cause on 4,138 death certificates. But it could be far worse as certificates are signed by physicians who have never seen the body, according to the *St Louis Post-Dispatch*.
www.seniorscopie.com

Angie Best, still stunning at 50.
Goodtimes magazine

3 DECEMBER 2002

Introducing Christina Aguilera, the *Top of the Pops* presenter said: "You'd better tell your grandma to leave the room." I thought this remark ageist until I saw the gross dancing and costume of Miss Aguilera. I did find her offensive, but not because I am an old prude. My 16-year-old granddaughter also finds the pop singer beyond crude. Next time the presenter should say: "Anyone who is civilised should leave the room."
Helen Webber, Forest Hill, southeast London

"I used to get the girl; now I get the part. In *The Quiet American* you may have noticed I got the part and the girl. It's a milestone for me, because it's the last time I'm going to get the girl. I'm sure of it, now I'm nearly 70."
Michael Caine in The Sunday Times Magazine

A fit, healthy and ruthless 74-year-old, I had no difficulty ensuring I was first on board the easyJet flight. I grabbed the

seat beside the emergency exit so that I would have extra room for my long, muscular legs. Along came a young air hostess: "Would you move to another seat, please? We want someone able-bodied sitting there." Some you win . . .
Dowie Cave, Holywood, Co Down

"Henry Kissinger, 79, returns from the political grave"
Front-page headline in The Guardian, Philip Stogdon, Crouch End, North London

10 DECEMBER 2002

As the blowsy, ballsy club singer Linda Green she's become a national sex symbol, but Liza Tarbuck says she's more of a cranky old lady – with a thing about litter. "The way I act sometimes, I could quite feasibly be a woman in my 60s or 70s," she says.
The Guardian

Alison Wilding, shortlisted for the Turner Prize in the 1980s and the early 1990s, never won; now, at 54, she is deemed too old to be a contender, irrespective of how her work may have matured.
Richard Cork in Tate magazine

Marcus Wareing, consultant chef of the soon-to-be refurbished Savoy Grill, suggests the makeover will be revolutionary. "I want it to be alive and exciting, not sad and boring. I'm 32 not 62," he says.
The Guardian

Major George Thom is one of nine finalists in the Grandparent of the Year Awards to be announced in London on Thursday. He keeps his local war memorial pristine – and teaches the bagpipes.

In the TV adaptation of *White Teeth*, Charles Collingwood (aka Brian Aldridge, who is currently embroiled in a steamy affair in *The Archers*) had a nude love scene with a young girl. "But I'm a gentleman of a certain age," he says bashfully, "and I prefer to do that kind of scene on radio where the audience can use their imagination."
The Observer

17 DECEMBER 2002

Theresa May (known for her snazzy shoes), the Conservative Party chairman, led the charge against Lord Heseltine, the former Deputy Prime Minister, saying that he should take up a new hobby. "I think he should take up golf, like every other retired person."
The Times

Paul Smith, the still-boyish 56-year-old . . .
Karen Kay, Evening Standard

"I'm a different guy here in my sixties. I don't have the same libido. It used to be that I didn't think I could go to sleep if I

wasn't involved in some kind of amorous contact. Well, I spend a lot of time sleeping alone these days."
Jack Nicholson, 65

For a man of his age – he will turn 73 next year – Clint Eastwood is showing no signs of slowing down. But that's not to say he doesn't look old. When he breaks into a smile, his face creases into a network of tiny lines, betraying his years.
Evening Standard

Baz Luhrmann is riveted by the fact of his having reached 40 in September. He is not depressed about entering his fifth decade. He insists – too much perhaps – that his 40th birthday was a welcome moment, when the priorities of physical pleasures give way to the spiritual. "Now, at 40, I have the right to say that I am a wise old man."
David Usborne, The Guardian

2003

7 JANUARY 2003

The rich imagination of Annie Proulx has made her books popular the world over – and yet she didn't finish her first novel until the age of 56.
Duncan Campbell, The Guardian

"Gee!" exclaimed the American tourist on entering the cathedral and admiring the pure Norman arches of the nave where I was on duty at the Welcomers' Desk. "How old is this place?" On learning that the first stone was laid in 1080, he gasped in awe. Then: "D'you mind if I take a photo of you? You look so authentic standing there." Agreed, I am 73, but *quand même . . .*
Nan Miller, Kent

Thigh-high boots are practically impossible to wear, and the
only women who try are dilapidated thirtysomething Sloanes
making one last stab at foxiness long after their legs have
gone.
The Sunday Times, from Mrs P.J. O'Brien, London N3

Whatever the Government says, older people at work are
widely considered, by their juniors, to be a faintly comical,
culpably unattractive, barely tolerable nuisance. That's why
there aren't any in the Cabinet.
Catherine Bennett, The Guardian

For some, this was a steep hill too many. Those with triple
chainsets and granny gears could take their time . . .
Cycle Touring & Campaigning, from F. M. Sonley, Skipton

Madonna: the queen of reinvention has come up trumps many
a time. But since moving to London her attire has become
dowdier. Has she finally decided to grow old gracefully?
The Times

Pete Waterman (55) is a bit old and tired now, desperately
clinging to his last chance at fame.
Louis Walsh in The Observer

14 JANUARY 2003

Modelling is like sport. At 30, you are dead. People get tired of
seeing the same old faces.
Carla Bruni, The Daily Telegraph

Avoid elasticated waistbands – you don't want to look like
you've strayed off an old biddies' package tour.
*Lisa Armstrong, The Times, sent in by Mary Fox, Carshalton, Surrey,
and others*

Bryan Ferry, 56, and his girlfriend, 21-year-old backing singer Kate Turner, were photographed enjoying themselves in the Caribbean. "It looked like a father and daughter on holiday together. Quite what she sees in him is anyone's guess, but it is certainly not his svelte figure."
Daily Mail

Richard Gere was still being voted the World's Sexiest Man and, despite his bifocals and greying hair, can by all accounts still arouse the odd frisson of excitement in the female breast.
BBC website, sent in by Paula Cenci, New York

I tried to buy a Dell computer system, requesting the 0 per cent finance advertised, but was told that they do not extend any finance arrangements to retired persons over 65. It is a long time since I have felt so angry and distressed over such an attitude. I am 68, with no mortgage and an impeccable credit rating.
John Humphreys, Southampton

There are agents and publishers who are prepared to put their faith in someone who is on the wrong side of 50. For a novelist to start after 50, and for people to believe in him, is fantastic.
Norman Lebrecht, winner of the Whitbread First Novel Award

21 JANUARY 2003

Kate O'Mara, 63, is best known for propelling her feline, high-cheek-boned beauty into a cheese-drenched acting career. She'd never admit it – but how many roles are there for Botox-enhanced sixtysomethings?
David Thomas, Daily Mail

Many of those in the 55–75 age group, dubbed the Goldies, are the ones having all the fun.
The Economic and Social Research Council

As a twentysomething it is hard to tell what is truly important above the noisy clatter of new releases, especially when *Friends* seems to be your only cultural compass. You can't ask your mother or father – they'd only start harking on about *On the Buses*.
Helen Rumbelow, The Times

David Beckham has lost his £1 million contract to promote Police sunglasses – and the man he has lost to is Hollywood hunk George Clooney. The former ER star may be 41, but he still has a lot going for him . . .
Sunday Mirror, sent in by Sue Brookshaw, Brighton

Headline in the *Daily Mail* over a story about the birth of Eric Clapton's new baby: Old Father Eric, 57
From Rose Miller, Lewisham, South London

An elderly woman was knocked down by a car at a pedestrian crossing in Woking town centre at lunchtime on Wednesday. The woman, aged 61 . . .
The Woking Review, from Miss E. Harrington, Beckenham, South London

28 JANUARY 2003

Dylan? The looks they are a-changing (and not for the better).
Daily Mail

Simon Hughes, MP for Bermondsey, has a real chance of becoming the next Mayor of London. He is over 50 – no spring chicken.
Simon Jenkins, Evening Standard

Sixty-year-old Britt Ekland is looking a trifle, well, Barbie-like in her dotage . . . Now for a woman of pensionable status, the

former Bond babe Ursula Andress clearly isn't your average old biddy down the bingo hall.
From Real, "the magazine for the modern thinking woman". From Eva Tenner, 75, London W12, "neither in my dotage nor an old biddy".

The time may come when maturity and constancy are valued above youngness, hipness and entrepreneurial flash, but it hasn't come yet.
Waldemar Januszczak, The Sunday Times

The emergence of knitting as an activity as attractive to men as to women may mark its transition from a soporific time-killer favoured by elderly ladies to a respectable hobby.
The Guardian

Perhaps it's something to do with the fact that, at 39 and expecting her third child, Sarah Lancashire knows there's little time left for her to bare all before everything starts moving south in a middle-aged slump.
The Eastern Daily Press Magazine, sent in by Professor Michael Balls, Norwich

I don't know if I'd go for an older man again. I found myself at cricket matches with people in their fifties.
Lowri Turner talking about her divorce to Paul Connew in the Daily Mail Weekend

4 FEBRUARY 2003

Whereas some middle-aged rock'n'roll singers have made the mistake of pretending that the clocks stopped ticking in 1970, Richard Thompson, 53, formerly of Fairport Convention, is finding that the genre responds well when the middle-aged embrace it on their terms.
Andrew Mueller, The Independent

He was much sought-after as a navigator and tactician, even in his sixties . . .
The Times obituary of Major Hugh Bruce, sent in by Peter Young, Cheltenham.

Age limits for the new rescue hovercraft will be 18 to 55. This extension from the normal inshore lifeboat retirement at 45 is due to the gentler ride provided by the hovercraft.
RNLI magazine, The Lifeboat, sent in by Dave Smithson, Brixham, Devon.

For years I have thought heathers were strictly for maiden aunts, grandmas or people who are entirely without taste.
Ann-Marie Powell, Amateur Gardening magazine, sent in by Mary Holterhoff, Lincoln.

For the mobile phone industry, the elderly (those aged 55 and over) are still a nascent market; most consider their mobile phones as a "glove box companion", bought for them by their concerned children. They keep them switched off and have to be encouraged to keep them on and use them, and know that texting is simple and nothing to be scared of.
New Media Age, sent in by Liz Coulson, Surbiton, southwest London.

11 FEBRUARY 2003

Baroness Williams of Crosby is expected to decide by the end of this week whether she is to stand as Chancellor of Oxford University. Some feel that her disastrous record as Education Secretary (she presided over the destruction of the grammar schools) ill-suits her to the job. Others feel that, at 73, she is too old.
Evening Standard

There was an extremely ageist cartoon* in *The Sunday Times* business section. It illustrates a letter asking for advice about

sacking someone who, at 62, is "a little old to do his job". The cartoon shows a painter, a client and a stooped old man shaking a tin of paint with squiggles indicating he is shaking all over, and the word "SHAKE" in capitals. The painter explains the old man to his client: "I just use him to mix the paint".
R. Thomas, Fareham, Hampshire. Because of copyright laws we are unable to reproduce the cartoon.

It is a cheerful thought that most young people today understand computer software far better than their elders, and they should grasp the point instantly. The present Luddism over genetic engineering may die a natural death as the computer-illiterate generation is superseded.
Professor Richard Dawkins, The Times, spotted by Joyce Glasser, Hampstead

My father celebrates his 70th birthday this year, and when I mentioned that this "milestone" deserves recognition, he replied that he now thinks of birthdays in metres rather than miles.
Julian Corlett, Scunthorpe

I'll save money for a rainy day when I'm really old, like 35 or something.
Shane from Westlife in Real magazine, sent in by Mrs I. Mottram, Hertfordshire

18 FEBRUARY 2003

I'm facing 30, but I'm not going to face wrinkles.
Natalie Imbruglia, in a L'Oreal advert. Sent in by Steve Williams, Epsom

SENIOR CITIZEN: Gimme my Discount!
T-shirt slogan spotted in Florida by Zena Nattriss of Reading, Berks

Die Hard 4: Die Hardest will also mark the return of Bruce Willis, now wheezing around the streets of New York at the age of 46.
The Observer, spotted by Mr A. W. Rogers, Richmond, Surrey

We were informed that the New Year's Eve entertainment would be in the form of a disco party, and it was felt that this would be unsuitable for our typical Countrywide customers, who are mostly 60-plus.
A holiday company justifies the absence of entertainment at a New Year's Eve function. Sent in by John Trewavas, Dorset

At the supermarket check-out I apologised for not hearing the till operator. I explained that I had a bit of a sore head after a Saturday night out, and joked that at my age, 57, I should know better than to overindulge. She said: "It's good that you manage to get out."
Jay Brooks, Warminster, Wilts

For our elders and betters: meals designed for and solely available to people over the age of 60. Any two meals for only £5.50.
Spotted in The White Hart pub by Mrs C. Benson of Wimborne, Dorset

On my 67th birthday last year, the traditional birthday cake was wheeled in with only four candles on it. When I queried the large shortfall in the number, my son replied: "We're counting down, not up."
David White Jones, Aylesbury, Bucks

25 FEBRUARY 2003

On a night out, Liz Hurley, 37, revealed more papery creases in her neck than her millionaire ex Steve Bing has in his money-clip.
News of the World

Before I turn 67, I would like to have a lot of sex with a man I like. If you want to talk first, Trollope works for me.
Personal ad in the New York Post reproduced in the Daily Mail

If there was one thing Dustin Hoffman (65) seemed guaranteed to have in later life, it was a glorious twilight of character parts.
Sean Macaulay, T2

This year I completed a 600-mile cycle journey. I was feeling smug until a lady in her middle years stood up and offered me a seat. It seems that you are as old as you look, not as old as you feel.
James Hopkins, 71, Preston

In the 12 months to March, two people over 65 were hospitalised after falling out of trees . . . a handful of people aged between 65 and 75 experienced falls involving ice skates, skis and skate-boards (and) one person over 60 had a fall "involving playground equipment".
A look at the causes of broken bones in Tayside, Scotland. Taken from The Courier, Dundee, by Tom Black, 67

Saddam is 65. How much longer can he live?
Robert Skidelsky, Prospect magazine. Sent in by Myrna Jacobs, London

Elderly tearaways, many of whom have had their driving licences suspended on medical grounds, have been accused of treating their electric scooters like "bumper cars".
The Times

4 MARCH 2003

Is Melanie Griffith losing her battle to hold back the years?
Daily Mail

When our daughter was seven we were discussing "in-laws". After explaining how Mummy's mother was my mother-in-law, I gave her a little test and said: "When you are grown up and have your own husband, what will I be?" Her response was: "Dead".

   I was then 55.
Ian Sheratte, London

"My job is a care worker dealing with old people over 45."
Contestant on Operatunity, C4. From Joan Wells, Rugby

Why do VIPs dress like OAPs?
T2 Headline. From Janet Wagon, Blewbury; Phil Jordan, Merseyside

Gail Hillman: "You were doing her a favour?"
   Richard: "What's she got to look forward to?"
   Gail: "She's 62!"
   Richard: "And her best years are behind her."
Coronation Street serial killer Richard tries to justify attempting to murder his mother-in-law. From Denis O'Donoghue, Bedfordshire

Romantic of the week: Police called to investigate noises coming from a car in Lanciano, Italy, discovered an 85-year-old man making love to his 74-year-old girlfriend. The man ran off, naked from the waist down.
The Sunday Times. From Judy Jesse, Flintshire

11 MARCH 2003

And when he has made the decision to go to war he will get permission from a reactionary old lady.
Beatrix Campbell talking about Tony Blair on Question Time. Sent in by Jane Kelly, London W8

My friend allowed her boyfriend to stay overnight. When I asked teasingly what the neighbours would think, she replied: "Oh, they wouldn't know. He parked his car round the corner and had to leave at 6am to get home before his mother woke up."

My friend's boyfriend is 64.
Mrs Vivienne Muir, Newcastle

Jilted Les Dennis, 48, was dumped by his lover, Leoni Cotgrove, 30, after her mother said he was too old.
The Sun

Short-fused supermodel Naomi Campbell appears to have given up her anger management course a trifle early. Her filthy mood swings are already alienating the domestic help at her New York apartment. The ageing catwalker . . .
Nigel Dempster, Daily Mail

DC Thomson, or DC's, as those of us who once worked there will always know this infuriating old woman of a company . . .
Euan Ferguson, The Observer

Dad dancing: Men over 30 should be banished from the dance floor, says Nick Foulkes.
The Sunday Times

My memory is going. I brush my teeth, and then ten minutes later I go back and have to feel the toothbrush. Is it wet? Did I just brush them? This whole mind that you've built up over years is developing moth holes.
Terry Gilliam, film-maker, 63, The Observer

18 MARCH 2003

My mum texts and she's over 50.
Victoria Derbyshire, Radio 5 Live presenter. Sent in by Harry Dutton, Radcliffe, Manchester

Police in Norway stopped Sigrid Krohn de Lange running down the street in Bergen because they thought that she had escaped from a nursing home. The 94-year-old jogger was out getting fit.
The Independent, Ireland. Sent in by Maedhbh McNamara, Dublin

I was shocked to read Oliver Del Mar's report, which compared Roy Keane's need for a hip replacement with that needed by "old women". He states: "In the case of old women, years spent shuffling to the bingo hall and back have climaxed in arthritis." As a youthful, sporty 53-year-old who needs a hip replacement, I found this comment ageist, sexist and breathtakingly ignorant.
Linda Carroll, Brighton

The blockbusters of today certainly offer more robust fare than the milksop films of 1971, tailored to meet the tastes of the very old or the very young: *The Railway Children*, *The Tales of Beatrix Potter*, *On the Buses* and *Up Pompeii*.
Times leader. Sent in by William Mosley, Liverpool

The author Paul Theroux explains why, even at the age of 61, his enthusiasm for female maturity remains undiminished.
T2, sent in by Freda Morton, Castletownroche, Co Cork

Setting off alone – and it's a brave 66-year-old woman who travels alone – Irma Kurtz retraced her footsteps, carefully noting the changes.
Val Hennessy, Daily Mail. Sent in by Jane R. Goodman, London N1

25 MARCH 2003

Actress Michelle Collins, 39, has come a long way since her days as stroppy Cindy Beale in *EastEnders*. She talks to Alix Miller about meditation and ageing gracefully.
Health & Fitness magazine. Sent in by Susan Debnam, Guildford, Surrey

We caught up with the women's caravan crossing the desert and we were surprised to see that there was even an elderly woman there of about 50.
Nicholas Middleton, author of Going to Extremes, speaking at the Royal Geographic Society. From Jane Kelly, West London

Sir Terence Conran, who, despite his 71 years, is no slouch when it comes to trendspotting, was definitely keeping up when he met with Britain's biggest furniture manufacturer.
Caroline Roux, The Guardian Weekend

Penny Lancaster, the latest RSB (Rod Stewart's Bird) bravely steps out in a black leather item fashioned from a Prada wallet and a lavatory chain. Clearly, with the old eyesight packing up, the RSB skirts need to get shorter and shorter if poor Rod is to see anything at all.
Allison Pearson, Evening Standard

My new wife is 32 and I'm 70. She's rejuvenated me totally. It's so exciting to see life through the eyes of a modern girl.
Wilbur Smith, Observer Magazine

I may not look 50, but I sure feel it. I'm worn out. Not physically. But the good thing about being 50 is thinking, "No I don't need to have a man around".
Marie Helvin, The Sunday Times

1 APRIL 2003

Gwen Taylor might be 64, but she is still offered plenty of acting roles.
Western Mail, sent in by Priscilla Stubbs, Pembrokeshire

Youngsters will watch crinklies if they're entertaining.
Tina Baker in TV Times, sent in by S. Hart, Southampton

There's no other way to put it: in pop music at the moment, old is the new new.
Mark Edwards, Culture, The Sunday Times

At a wartime dance a devastatingly handsome pilot and I were getting to know each other. He said he was 18. I confessed to being 21. "Never mind, you don't look it," he said. I recall thinking "I'll see the funny side of that when I'm old and 40". I'm over 80 and it still makes me smile.
Geraldine Ash, Hatherleigh, Devon

John Oxford, a professor of virology at Queen Mary School of Medicine, London, says that as a weapon, even smallpox has its limitations: "It is like a pensioner. It is such a plodder . . ."
The Guardian

Am I, at 31, too old to be fashionable?
Melinda Stevens, Style, The Sunday Times

This journey would be hard on any traveller: for one aged 60, it is a major achievement.
Review of Paul Theroux's Dark Star Safari. Sent in by C. E. Robins, Norwich

8 APRIL 2003

Carol Channing, 82, famous for her Broadway hit *Hello, Dolly!*, wrote about her first love, Harry Kullijian, in her autobiography. Widower Harry, 83, read the book, phoned up his teenage sweetheart and now the two are engaged.
The Miami Herald

Anyone who saw Tony Blair in the Commons yesterday would have been struck that, for a man whose 50th birthday is little more than a month away, he still looks remarkably good.
Tom Baldwin, The Times. Sent in by several readers

The aeroplane is full of awayday passengers, mostly over 50. Although a guided tour is on offer for part of the day, the girls make a mental note not to get stuck with the "Bettys".
Times Educational Supplement

Community activist Cathy McCormack, now 50, but as tightly sprung and chirpy as a woman half her age . . .
The Big Issue, Scotland. Sent in by Marjory Grant, Edinburgh

Tony Blackburn is in the middle of one of the most unexpected comebacks since Christ. He is absolutely loving his reinvention at the advanced age of 60.
Marianne Macdonald, Evening Standard. Sent in by Dennis Smith, Chessington, Surrey

In trim shape, with close-cropped greying hair, Rowan Atkinson looks good for his 48 years.
The Times Magazine, sent in by Michael Henderson, Westward Ho

15 APRIL 2003

Geri-atric – with parched skin and wrinkles round the eyes it looks like Geri Halliwell has been enjoying the Californian sun a little too much. Either that or the sprightly singer is succumbing to the effects of ageing. She is 30, after all.
The Sun. Sent in by Neil Hazlehurst, Windermere

The old boy is probably wise to be getting as much mileage as he can out of looking artlessly dishevelled.
Jane Shilling, writing about Hugh Grant, 42. Sent in by Anthony Bleakley, Poole

A summer evening dress with sleeves is easy to find, if you don't mind looking mumsy.
The Sunday Times Style

Wilbur Smith, 70, revealed his 92-year-old mother's attitude to age on BBC Radio Leeds. She says: "The paint and plaster may be peeling and cracking on the outside but that doesn't matter if the rooms inside are warm and cosy."
From Peter Rushforth, Bradford

The stubble may be greying but Andre Agassi shows no signs of ageing. The 32-year-old is playing with a youthful verve.
The Times. Sent in by Liz McIntosh, Dundee

There are continuing rumours that Heather Mills McCartney is pregnant despite the fact that her husband is 60.
Lynda Lee-Potter, Daily Mail. Sent in by Andrew Hall, Southend

22 APRIL 2003

Tracey Emin will be 40 in July. But she claims she isn't bothered.
Marianne Macdonald, Evening Standard

Martha Lane Fox was whisked on to *Question Time*, such was the desire of the producer to present someone who was a woman who didn't look like your granny.
Chris Blackhurst, Evening Standard, sent in by Raymond McCann, London

I try to go to Mass every week and because I am 40 I stand out. The congregation is mostly grey-haired. I don't want guitars and dancing, but it would be good to feel part of something alive.
Sophie Pierce, The Daily Telegraph

Cellulite is the scourge of women who aren't as young as they once were. It says: "Look, you've got old, and it's all downhill from here."
Shane Watson, The Sunday Times Style

Mark Ellen, ex-bass player of Ugly Rumours, Tony Blair's band at university, says ten years ago people who commissioned became young. "Before that, in the BBC, you always suspected the hierarchy went home and listened to tea dances."
The Guardian

When I was young I paid more regard to intellect than judgment. As I've got older I pay more regard to judgment than intellect.
Tony Blair, Saga Magazine

29 APRIL 2003

People are always talking about when the Rolling Stones should retire, but it's a racial thing. Nobody ever says B. B. King is too old to play. It's like you can't be white and be an old rock'n'roller.
David Bailey, Vogue

Richard to Judy on Paul Newman: "Doesn't he look incredible, given that he's 77."
Sent in by Graeme Forster

Oxford University's new Chancellor, Chris Patten, is still active at 58.
The Spectator, sent in by D. Smith, Chessington

Top 10 work goals to achieve in your 40s:
   1. Show that you are not too old to learn.
From an advert for the Government-supported Learndirect. Sent in by Joyce Glaser, London

Arnold Schwarzenegger, 55, will reprise his rusty robot role in *Terminator 3* . . . there will be competition from Sylvester

Stallone, 56, in *Rambo IV*, and Bruce Willis, a youthful 48, is filming *Die Hard 4*. Pass the Magnum and wrinkle cream.
Andrew Pierce, The Times

Calvin Klein had to be escorted from a basketball game in New York. Amelia Torode, of the Headlight global trends firm, thinks people might have thought the bad-boy image witty and eccentric when he was 40, but as an older man it looks a bit sad.
The Guardian

6 MAY 2003

It was a great game, and I thought what I always think when I watch Manchester United. Where else can you see a 61-year-old man chewing gum?
Frank Skinner in The Times, on Sir Alec Ferguson. From Anthony Bleakley, Poole

Poets aren't respected until they're in their fifties and they've honed their craft. It's odd that pop music goes the other way.
Singer Lucinda Williams, 50, The Guardian

Women over 45 feel more confident sexually than when they were younger and are more likely to try to hang from the chandeliers than their offspring.
Colette Harris, Health Plus

My biology teacher friend described the human sex act to a class of pupils aged 15 to 16. A voice called out: "My Mum and Dad still do it and they're 50." The entire class let out a "Yuck". My friend, 50, could only smile.
Pam Cheshire, Nottingham

The trend of agelessness has never been so relevant, yet so often ignored. Most marketers fall into the pitfall of aggregating

anyone over 50 into a single pot and missing lots of opportunities as well as alienating a large number of consumers.
Marketing report by The Henley Centre

Nowadays Chrissie Hynde says she's content "just getting old and being in a great rock band".
   She is 52.
The Independent

13 MAY 2003

Still a working designer at 63, Zandra Rhodes hails from a time altogether more fabulous than ours.
Evening Standard

Listeners who miss a BBC radio show can download it. You need the RealOne Player and must identify yourself, with name, address and age. The system offers a choice – but not for anyone born before 1940.
From Gordon Sapsed, Southampton

National Outdoor Week offers the chance to try outdoor sports, from gentle pursuits such as walking and cycling for the over-fifties, to adventures such as white-water rafting and mountaineering.
Sunday Times Travel Section, from James Tolson, Arundel

Most grandmothers spend time knitting, settling down with a book or going for a stroll. But 71-year-old Erika Erla is disproving this image – by making waves in the world of powerboat racing.
The Bucks Herald, sent in by Margaret Ross, Aylesbury

"At the age of 37/ She realised she'd never ride/ Through Paris, in a sports car/ With the warm wind in her hair." It's from

a song called *The Ballad of Lucy Jordan*, which was recorded
by Marianne Faithfull. I've always loathed it.
Sent in by David Bailey

20 MAY 2003

We want to make movies that can attract an older audience for
whom many films are not appealing. David Thompson, head of
BBC Films, on *The Mother*, featuring Anne Reid as a 65-year-
old who has an affair with her daughter's boyfriend.
The Sunday Times

Now Charlotte Rampling is nearing 60 and reaching the stage
in her career when life should mean comfortable cardigans and
the odd role playing someone's granny.
Valentine Low, Evening Standard

I'm the living proof that you can fall in love like a teenager,
even at 62.
   Theatre producer Greg Smith talking of his new paramour,
singer Shirley Bassey, 63.
Daily Mail

Men look rubbish by the time they hit 40, all pink and swaddled
in fat from too many business lunches and after-work lagers.
Tim Lott, Evening Standard

Despite the occasional wheeze, Harrison Ford, 60, showed he
was up to the task of playing with Liam, two-year-old adopted
son of Calista Flockhart.
Daily Mail

Andrew Cracknell, 56, is one of the oldest creative chiefs in
London. That he has survived well beyond the natural lifespan
of most people working in advertising ...
Campaign, sent in by Reg Starkey (62), London

27 MAY 2003

Has Trevor Brooking found a new vocation late in life?
Niall Quinn, recently retired player and now pundit on Sky TV.
Brooking is 52. Sent in by John Hall, Basingstoke

Bob Clark, director of education of Wigan, has announced he
is retiring at the tender age of 55. But he has no intention of
abandoning the world of education, and certainly not of opting
full-time for slippers and gardening.
Times Educational Supplement

Elle Macpherson's youthful appearance is all the more
remarkable given she is 38.
Marianne Macdonald, Evening Standard

After an "absolutely terrifying" entrance exam and interview,
retired high court judge Sir Oliver Popplewell was told he had a
place at Harris Manchester College, Oxford, to read PPE with
the admonition that students are expected to contribute
something to society. He said, "I will be 79 when I leave so I'm
going to be fairly old and I'll have already made my
contribution to society."
The Guardian

Men in their early 40s are prone to unusual behaviour.
Alex Wade, The Guardian

I don't think anybody around today will be around for 40 years
like I have. Not because of lack of talent, but because artists
are created with a shelf-life of about three or four years.
Gene Pitney, The Guardian

3 JUNE 2003

The French actress Emmanuelle Béart, on appearing in *Elle* in the nude: "It showed that a woman, any woman, is still a woman at 37 years old."
The Sunday Times, sent in by Derek Williams, Swansea

Extract from interview with *Sun* Page 3 model Charlotte:
    Q: How old are you? A: 21.
    Q: Where do you see yourself in five years? A: I'll still be modelling if I can keep the wrinkles at bay.
Alan Guthrie, Cardiff

There's a generational divide between briefs and thongs and I'm depressingly aware that I'm on the oldies' side.
Alexandra Shulman, The Daily Telegraph

JUST A THONG AT TWILIGHT

"We have a kind of golden market for the over-55s now . . . eyesight willing."
Mark McCallum, marketing director of Random House, on "Granny Lit"

From a course syllabus by Bracknell and Wokingham College, Berkshire: "Move into Fitness for the Over-50s – Try a fitness session for the less mobile."
Graham Langley, Crowthorne

Overheard in the office: "So, this press-up, is it an exercise for elderly people?" "No, it's for normal people."
Miriam Harper, Hemel Hempstead

Doug Ellis, chairman of Aston Villa FC, is 79. He is a relic from the Dark Ages.
Arlo White, Radio 5 Live sports presenter. Sent in by Harry Dutton, Manchester

10 JUNE 2003

Getting older is fabulous, says Cherie Lunghi, 51. "The longer you do it, the more technique you acquire. That makes the game easier."
Evening Standard

When a play calls itself *The Vagina Monologues* you can be pretty sure it is not for your maiden aunt. The audience that had come to see it at the New Victoria Theatre, Woking, was 90 per cent female, and most of them on the right side of 50.
Surrey Advertiser, sent in by Sue Camp (the wrong side of 50), Cranleigh, Surrey

Tristram Hunt, the Civil War historian, should look more fetching in a black leather jacket than Simon Schama, 58, who has graced our screens with marvellous commentary but slightly too much narcissism for his advancing years.
Camilla Cavenish, The Times

We condemn young fathers for failing to live up to their responsibilities, yet have nothing but well wishes for old ones

like Paul McCartney who simply won't live long enough to fulfil theirs.
Amanda Platell, Evening Standard

I'd love to meet the right bloke, settle down, have a family. I'm 32 this year and could end up an old woman with cats, smelling of cat's pee, if I'm not careful.
Jessie Wallace, aka Kat Slater of EastEnders, The Sun

17 JUNE 2003

You would never think Jean Paul Gaultier was 50. The hair might be grey rather than blond, the eyes a little less periwinkle blue, but he is too full of childlike exuberance to look his age.
Laura Craik, Evening Standard

Registering to order a book on www.swotbooks.com, I was asked for my age from the menu which read:
   Under 20 Under 30 Under 40 Jolly Old
Annabel Davis, Heston, Middlesex

Until I hit 70, I'm not gonna start partying again. I'll wait until I'm really old, then I'll start taking acid again.
Evan Dando, rock singer and reformed substance abuser, in the New York Post.

Two old men were sitting in the reading room and one said to the other: "You're 82 years old, how do you honestly feel?" "Honestly, I feel like a newborn baby," answered the other. "I've got no hair, no teeth, and I just wet myself."
From the Civil Service Pensioner's "Chuckle Corner", June 2003. Submitted by Gerald Morris, Edinburgh

Should women over 25 wear miniskirts?
Headline in the Daily Express, June 13, 2003

The Welsh mum has been married for 30 years and despite concerns that her reflection is a sad, saggy ghost of her younger self, she still remembers the petite younger artist, every inch of her oozing glamour.
From an interview with the artist Erica Evans, 52, in the Western Mail, June 10

They really do look like grandpa. They have thinning hair and wrinkles.
Dr Audie Leventhal, of the University of Utah School of Medicine, who studies 30-year-old macaques in Kunming, China

24 JUNE 2003

"Barry Manilow, 60 today and still going strong. Amazing!"
Ed Stewart on Radio 2.
Sent in by Terry Western, Sudbury, Suffolk

"Now, in *Basic*, he looks better than he has done in years, despite the fact that he's 49."
Grace Bradberry on John Travolta in the Daily Mail's Weekend magazine.
Sent in by Jo Collins, Oxford

"Who doesn't remember the national debate when the thong first arrived on the scene? Incredible now to think that a style that has become de rigueur for women under 50 could have caused such a diversion."
The Sunday Times Style magazine, sent in by Anon (who declares: "Yes, I wear a thong; yes, I'm over 50; no, it doesn't look hideous")

A lady in a local cafe this morning excitedly told the young waitress about her summer holiday destination. The waitress replied: "Oh, I went there last year. For people my age it was really too quiet, but you'll be in heaven."
Julian Corlett, Scunthorpe

"It's a sign of age when the back of your head looks better than the front."
Overheard in a hairdressing establishment by Barry Young, Cleveland

"Should T-shirts with slogans be worn by the over-thirties?"
James Delingpole in T2, June 17

"My eldest son is about to become 21, and all I can say is that he makes me feel incredibly old. He is an incredible help and assistance to me as I become increasingly decrepit."
The Prince of Wales talks about his elder son, Prince William, in the Yorkshire Post

1 JULY 2003

Aside from the thinning hair and expanding waistline, what should be worrying Chris Evans now is . . .
Thomas Sutcliffe, The Independent

If everyone over 55 takes the "polypill", a combination of drugs which would prevent a heart attack and stroke, a third would gain an average of 12 years.
Professor Nicholas Wald, The Times

Club owner Peter Stringfellow, 62, says he does not want to live until he is 120 – unless he can still have sex.
The Sun

Babes miss out as US lusts for sirens over 40.
Headline in The Sunday Times

Don't let Andre Agassi's age, 33, put you off – he's as fit now as he's ever been, and an acute ability to pick his tournaments carefully means he's always in great shape.
The Game (from The Times), sent in by Hazel Grainger, Marshland St James, Norfolk

Jockey Mick Kinane is in his fifth year at the Co Tipperary stable and has played a full part in the unparalleled success of trainer Aidan O'Brien. At 44, however, there are those who feel his strongest and sharpest days are behind him.
Alan Lee/Chris McGrath, The Times, sent in by Peter Leighton, Cannock, Staffs

8 JULY 2003

"As I get older I try to seize the day more than I ever did, because there is more gone than there is to come."
Maggie Smith, Evening Standard

"I'd like to see a version of *Big Brother* made with 'oldie' contestants – say 55 to 65 . . . of course, the tasks would have to be simpler: perhaps a knitting contest or best sardonic answers to questions in the diary room."
Letter in the Radio Times, sent in by Philippa Russell, Birmingham, and Annabel Henfrey, Tarporley, Cheshire

"As you get older, it is easier for a young girl to lead you astray."
A solicitor explains why his client was caught bringing drugs into the UK. John Randall, 65, from Norfolk, had agreed to carry suitcases of "clothes and gifts" for a young Jamaican woman.

What editor can be bothered any more with arm-wrestling publicists for passé Hollywood royals like Tom Cruise and Penelope Cruz? That relationship has no sizzle anyway. At 41 he's too old (outside the demo, as MTV would say) . . .
Tina Browne, T2

15 JULY 2003

The real revelation in *The Look of Love* is Meg Ryan. It is no secret that most of us thought she had passed her sell-by date.
Baz Bamigboye, Daily Mail

Both Carol Smillie, 42, and 47-year-old Jerry Hall belied their ages in revealing holiday bikinis.
Fiona Cummins, Daily Mirror

Melanie Griffith has taken over the role of Roxie Hart in *Chicago* on Broadway. When the 45-year-old star lost the Revlon contract, she commented: "I'm too old for 'defy it'. I mean, now I'm like, 'F**k it'."
Evening Standard

The Osmonds are back in the charts after 20 years – but what a heavy toll those years have taken on the daddy of all boy bands.
Daily Mail

Jay Haas is more competitive than ever. At 49, an age when bodies break down and minds begin to wander, Haas has found the proverbial second wind.
GolfWorld, sent in by M. E. McLoughlin, London

The dressing room could be used as a fifth bedroom, but only for an uncomplaining child or a grandparent.
The Times, Bricks and Mortar, sent in by Julia Shipton, Exeter

The main reason everyone is talking about Ashton Kutcher is because he is the "toy boy" lover of the fabulous but nonetheless 40-year-old Demi Moore.
Jane Bussmann, Evening Standard

22 JULY 2003

Anyone harbouring visions of Erica Jong sitting in a rocking chair, knitting baby booties, should get over it. At 61, she is still as lusty and provocative as the woman who penned the phrase "the zipless f***" three decades ago.
Sharon Krum, The Guardian

Jeremy Clarkson is . . . decades past his sell-by date.
Victor Lewis-Smith, Evening Standard

Honest John (*Daily Telegraph*) replying to a 71-year-old's query about buying a car with automatic transmission: "A switch to automatic at your age would be dangerous . . . because it is easy to become confused and lose control."
Douglass Sparling, Thurso.

The convention on Europe's future packed its bags last week in Brussels. At one of the many events to celebrate its achievements, Valéry Giscard d'Estaing, an elderly former President of France, was asked to address an organisation called Friends of Europe. With unintentional irony, the event was held in the dinosaurs' hall of the Natural History Museum in Brussels. The image of a 77-year-old man standing in front of a diplodocus was uncomfortably apt.
The Economist

"We think Patsy Kensit is not looking too bad at all for a 35-year-old working single mum-of-two."
Western Mail, sent in by Priscilla Stubbs, Pembroke

29 JULY 2003

This year Brad Pitt will turn 40. He claims to be undaunted . . .
Martyn Palmer, The Sunday Times Culture

When I was 47 I asked a young lady whether all her cruise liner's cabins had bunk beds adding, to explain my concern, that the proposed trip was to celebrate our silver wedding. She was quick to reassure me that, though this was the case, "they are quite low so you shouldn't have any trouble getting in and out of them".
Mary Cottrill, Lymm, Cheshire

Apparently more than 80 per cent of open-top sports cars are sold to sad sacks who believe this throbbing mechanical extension makes them look young and virile, not old and desperate.
Amanda Craig, The Sunday Times

There's great relief in being middle-aged that, although you look rubbish, everyone else does, too. Ageing is the most democratic force in the universe.
Tim Lott, Evening Standard

Rumour has it there is another *Indiana Jones* film proposed and that Harrison Ford, 61, is to play the part again – no doubt with a bathchair in the wings.
Simon Bates, Classic FM, sent in by Dr Peter Lewis (age 71), Tenterden, Kent

Here is proof that no one makes the case for natural boobs better than Madonna. At 44, she may be getting on a bit . . .
The Sun

5 AUGUST 2003

"When you get to a certain age you are offered only old-bag roles. I have sung all the leading soprano roles there are and I don't want to end up singing old-bag roles."
Dame Anne Evans, 61, on her imminent retirement

Steven Berkoff is still angry, and still craving attention at 65. So when is this teenage delinquent going to grow up?
Rachel Cooke, ES magazine

Sex and the City star Kim Cattrall has complained that she is finding it hard to get a date. Well, dear, it's what you should expect at 46. As we get older we all begin to have difficulty with dates, names, where we parked . . .
The Sunday Times, sent in by John Blasby, East Sussex

I'm trying to capture a specific moment, in a club or pub, a reflection of Birmingham. I can't see it appealing to the post-40 generation, who tend to like Monets and watercolours.
The artist Jane Anderson, Birmingham Post, sent in by Joan Bates, Edgbaston

Entry for Jeffrey Simmons, literary agent, in *Writer's Handbook 2003*. Interests: fiction from young writers (ie, under 40) with a future.
Sent in by Richard Tapsfield, Tunbridge Wells

Nikki Page, John Redwood's new friend, and I hit it off in the dusty world of Tory politics: neither of us had blue hair and we were both under 70.
Amanda Platell, formerly William Hague's spin-doctor

12 AUGUST 2003

Commenting on an Yves Saint Laurent ad for scent, *The Sunday Times* says: At 37, Emmanuelle Seigner looks great naked.
Sent in by Ernest Caspari, Newnham, Gloucestershire

A bunch of pensioners shaking off the cobwebs to embark on their upteenth round-the-world trip could rightfully be expected to be rather out ot touch with what young people are listening

to. But the Rolling Stones' choice of support acts for their current world tour has revealed a healthy interest in the youthful pretenders to their throne.
David Smyth, Evening Standard

I get to meet a lot of really neat older people. Women who are, like, 30.
Singer Amanda Bynes, 17, sent in by Gresham Cooke, London W8

Now a doting grandmother of two, Felicity Kendal still made it on to a list of Top Ten TV Sex Bombs.
Maureen Paton, The Daily Telegraph

Isn't it unnerving to be filming sex scenes at 53? Jasper Gerard, of *The Sunday Times*, wanted to know of Julie Walters, one of the stars of *Calendar Girls*.
Sent in by Mrs Jill Peel (aged 67), Carnforth, Lancs

Shirley Valentine star Tom Conti is making a comeback – at 62.
Daily Express, sent in by Mrs E. McLintock, Glasgow

19 AUGUST 2003

Everyone has to go through a rebellious period, and at least I did it in my early thirties rather than having a mid-life crisis at 40. That would have been really embarrassing.
Rachel Hunter, The Sun

The gods, deprived of Freia's youth-giving apples, stoop and age and sit in a gloomy row like pensioners on the Hastings seafront.
Robert Thicknesse reviewing Wagner, The Times

Arnold Schwarzenegger, currently hoping to be the next Governor of California, has shown (despite having heart surgery in 1997) that you can be fit in your 50s.
Gavin Evans, The Guardian

I'm definitely going to buy a Ferrari soon. I think it's good to treat yourself occasionally – after all there's no point in driving a Ferrari when you're 60.
Lord Raj Sharma in the Daily Mail, sent in by Mrs Janet Alldread, Beckenham, Kent

In older women, a style rut is forgivable. Joan Collins, Shirley Bassey and Cilla Black haven't changed their image since the dawn of time.
Laura Craik, Evening Standard

She may have reached 30, but Cameron Diaz has a figure that would be the envy of women half her age.
Now magazine, sent in by Sophie Starkey, Cheltenham, Gloucestershire

INDEX